CW00662595

Discovery Walks Around the Welsh Borders

Brian Conduit

Meridian Books

Published 2008 by Meridian Books

© Brian Conduit 2008

ISBN 978-1-869922-58-0

A catalogue record for this book is available from the British Library.

The right of Brian Conduit to be identified as author of this book has been asserted by him in accordance with the Copyright, Designs and Patents Act 1988.

All rights reserved. No part of this publication may be copied, reproduced or transmitted in any form or by any means without the prior written permission of the publishers.

Meridian Books
8 Hartside Close, Lutley, Halesowen, West Midlands B63 1HP

Printed in Great Britain by Cromwell Press, Trowbridge, Wiltshire

Contents

The glorious ruins of Tintern Abbey
Walk 18

Illustrations

Introduction

In the eighth century the Anglo-Saxon king Offa the Great, ruler of Mercia, constructed a dyke along the length of his western borders between his territories and those of the Welsh princes. It ran from the mouth of the Dee in the north to the mouth of the Wye in the south, on or close to the modern English-Welsh border.

By any criteria it was a tremendous feat of construction. Although purely an earthwork, with no evidence of any stone structures anywhere along its length, it certainly ranks with Hadrian's Wall which it considerably exceeds in length. However unlike Hadrian's Wall, we know very little about its construction and its exact purpose remains a matter of conjecture. The absence of any fortifications tends to suggest that it was not intended primarily for defence but was probably built as a boundary marker and perhaps to act as some kind of regulated crossing point. Throughout Anglo-Saxon England there are plenty of other, somewhat shorter examples of linear earthworks built to mark boundaries between various tribal kingdoms and territories.

It seems likely therefore that Offa's Dyke represents the first attempt to define the frontier between the Anglo-Saxon English and Celtic Welsh. It passes through and overlooks some of the most glorious, dramatic and unspoilt countryside in the whole of Britain and, as any walker knows, it has become the focal point of a popular national trail. On its route from Prestatyn to Chepstow, Offa's Dyke Path keeps to the line of the dyke itself wherever this is known and possible – about 30 miles (55km) of its 177 mile (285km) length – and in some places substantial stretches of the dyke can still be seen snaking across the border terrain. Inevitably some of the walks in this guide make use of stretches of the path which has the advantages of being well-waymarked, as indeed are most of Britain's national trails, and taking you through some outstanding scenery. At the same time, while revealing these superb landscapes, it also takes you up and down some pretty steep hillsides.

Hills are indeed the chief ingredient of the Welsh Border country. Even when walking in the flattish and gently undulating countryside of north Shropshire and parts of Herefordshire, the hills are always on the horizon. The steep-sided slopes of the South Shropshire Hills – which include the Long Mynd, Wenlock Edge and Clee Hills – are excellent walking country and provide a series of extensive views both eastwards over the Midlands and westwards towards the hills of mid-Wales. This was the countryside that was so loved by A.E. Housman, author of *A Shropshire Lad*.

Further south after flowing through the gentle and lush dairy pastures of Herefordshire, the River Wye does a series of wide loops, narrows to a gorge and in the lower part of its valley continues between steep-sided and thickly wooded banks, finally disgorging into the Bristol Channel just beyond the massive border castle at Chepstow. In the late eighteenth and early nineteenth centuries, the dramatic scenery, spectacular viewpoints such as Symonds Yat, and picturesque ruins of this area – the castles at Goodrich and Chepstow and the remains of Tintern Abbey in their incomparable riverside setting – attracted many of the writers, artists and painters of the 'Romantic' era, like Wordsworth and Turner. They and the increasing number of later visitors would do the 'Wye Tour', hiring boats from Ross-on-Wye and travelling down this magnificent stretch of river to Monmouth and on to Chepstow.

One feature that you would expect to find in any border zone are castles and a large number of defensive structures and fortifications of all kinds – large or small, complete or derelict, semi-ruinous or, in some cases, little more than a few bumps in the ground – litter the Welsh Border. They range from prehistoric hill forts and Norman motte and bailey castles to the mighty medieval fortresses built by the Marcher Lords. The Marcher Lords were a group of barons, granted semi-independent powers by William the Conqueror and his successors in return for defending the border and keeping the Welsh under control. These ruthless and ambitious men – principally the Earls of Chester, Shrewsbury, Hereford and Gloucester – used their power to gain the maximum land, wealth and influence for themselves. In time they became as much of a threat to the king, their master and employer, as to the Welsh princes, their supposed enemies, often switching allegiances and constantly scheming in order to enhance their wealth and power. The eventual completion of the conquest of Wales by Edward I in the late thirteenth century considerably reduced the power of these Marcher Lords and rendered many of their great castles almost obsolete. Finally the Acts of Union with Wales (1536-42) abolished their authority by adding the Marcher lands to the existing counties and creating a new government body, the Council of Wales, which was based at Ludlow Castle.

As well as grand views and mighty castles, the Welsh Border country also possesses some of the most delightful old towns in the country – Shrewsbury, Ludlow, Ross-on-Wye, Monmouth, and Chepstow to name a few – and a number of unspoilt and attractive villages. All these have pubs, guest houses and bed and breakfast establishments that provide excellent bases from which to explore this fascinating area. In an age of noise and bustle, much of the countryside on the English-Welsh border has a quiet and pleasant off the beaten track feel, something which it is becoming increasingly harder to find. The best way to experience this elusive commodity and enjoy the landscapes that inspired, among many others, Housman, Turner and Wordsworth, is to put on your boots and start walking.

Brian Conduit, 2008

The Routes

The majority of walks in this guide fall within the moderate to easy categories and are well within the capabilities of most walkers. There are just a few that are more strenuous and involve some steep climbing. Look at the general descriptions of each walk carefully and note the brief details on terrain before deciding which of them suit you best, depending on your preferences, how far you want to go, the time that you have available and your level of fitness.

All are on public rights of way or permissive routes, such as paths across National Trust land, Forestry Commission trails and canal towpaths. Road walking is kept to a minimum and is mainly confined to quiet country lanes. Where stretches of main road are unavoidable, there is always a pavement or grass verge.

Every effort has been made to ensure that descriptions are correct and the routes have been carefully checked. However, no guarantees can be given that they are error free and that there are no misprints or inaccuracies.

The routes should be easy to follow, although you are advised to take with you the appropriate Ordnance Survey Explorer map. If while on a public footpath you encounter obstacles which make your passage difficult, report any such problems to the Rights of Way department of the relevant local authority (addresses on page 9).

Maps

The sketch maps are intended as a guide and not to replace Ordnance Survey maps which, together with a compass and some basic

Shrewsbury Abbey

Walk 3

first aid, you should always have with you. Although I hope this will not happen, there is always the possibility that you might need to change your route because of bad weather or some unexpected incident. Maps should preferably be the Explorer series which are much more useful to walkers than Landrangers.

The following Explorer maps cover the walks in this guide: 240 (Oswestry), 241 (Shrewsbury), 201 (Knighton & Presteigne), 216 (Welshpool & Montgomery), 217 (The Long Mynd & Wenlock Edge), 203 (Ludlow), 202 (Leominster & Bromyard), OL13 (Brecon Beacons National Park – Eastern area) and OL14 (Wye Valley & Forest of Dean)

Useful addresses and websites

The Ramblers' Association, 2nd Floor, Camelford House, 87-90 Albert Embankment, London SE1 7TW
Tel: 020 7339 8500. www.ramblers.org.uk

The National Trust, PO Box 39, Warrington WA5 7WD
Tel: 0870 458 4000. www.nationaltrust.org.uk

Local Authorities

Shropshire County Council, Shirehall, Abbey Foregate, Shrewsbury SY2 6ND
Tel: 0845 678 9000 www.shropshire.gov.uk

Herefordshire County Council, Brockington, 35 Hafod Road, Hereford HR1 1SH

Tel: 01432 260000 www.herefordshire.gov.uk

Gloucestershire County Council, Shire Hall, Gloucester GL1 2TG
Tel: 01452 425000 www.gloucestershire.gov.uk

Powys County Council, County Hall, Llandrindod Wells, Powys LD1 5LG
Tel: 0845 055 2155 www.powys.gov.uk

Monmouthshire County Council, County Hall, Cwmbran, Monmouthshire NP44 2XH
Tel: 0001633 644644 www.monmouthshire.gov.uk

Local Tourist Information Centres

England

Oswestry Tel: 01691 622753 ot@oswestry-welshborders.org.uk
Shrewsbury Tel: 01743 281200 tic@shrewsburytourism.co.uk
Church Stretton Tel: 01694 723133 churchstretton.scf@shropshire.gov.uk
Craven Arms Tel: 01588 676000 secret.hills@shropshire-cc.gov.uk
Ludlow Tel: 01584 875053 ludlow.tourism@shropshire.gov.uk
Leominster Tel: 01568 616460 tic-leominster@herefordshire.gov.uk

Queenswood Country Park Tel: 01568 797842
  queenswoodtic@herefordshire.gov.uk
Hereford Tel: 01432 268430 tic-hereford@herefordshire.gov.uk
Ross-on-Wye Tel: 01989 562768 tic-ross@herefordshire.gov.uk
Newent Tel: 01531 822468 newent@fdean.gov.uk
Coleford Tel: 01594 812388 tourism@fdean.gov.uk

Wales

Welshpool Tel: 01938 552043 weltic@powys.gov.uk
Knighton Tel: 01547 529424 oda@offasdyke.demon.co.uk
Hay-on-Wye Tel: 01497 820144 post@hay-on-wye.co.uk
Monmouth Tel: 01600 713899 monmouth.tic@monmouthshire.gov.uk
Chepstow Tel: 01291 623772 chepstow.tic@monmouthshire.gov.uk

Public Transport

For information about bus and train services either phone Traveline on 0870 6082608 or visit the website www.traveline.org.uk
Alternatively contact the local tourist information centre.

Stokesay Castle
Walk 8

About the author

Brian Conduit was born and bred in Birmingham, went to school there and obtained a B.A.Hons. degree in Medieval and Modern History from Birmingham University in 1960. He became a history teacher, first in Buckinghamshire but mainly in Lancashire where he has have lived for over 40 years, although still retaining many connections with the Midlands. While teaching in Lancashire he began writing walking guides and after taking early

retirement in 1995 concentrated full time on writing. For many years he was Series Consultant and principal author of the Pathfinder walking guides published by Jarrold

He has written over 40 books, plus articles on history and walking for *History Today, The Great Outdoors, Footloose, Outdoor, Country Walking.* He has also presented five series of walking programmes, *Walking through History*, on Radio Lancashire 1984-89.

Also by the author:

Walking through History (Constable 1983)

Exploring Sherwood Forest (Dalesman 1985)

Walks from your Car – Sherwood Forest (Dalesman 1988)

Heritage Trails in North West England (Cicerone 1989)

Walking in Warwickshire (Cicerone 1998)

Discovery Walks in Lancashire (Sigma 1999)

Discovery Walks in Worcestershire (Sigma 2000)

Discovery Walks in Birmingham and the Black Country (Sigma 2001)

Battlefield Walks in the Midlands (Sigma 2004)

Battlefield Walks: Northumbria and the Scottish Borders (Sigma 2005)

Short Walks – Sussex and South Downs (Jarrold 2003)

Short Walks – South Devon (Jarrold 2004)
Walks into History: Lancashire (Countryside 2006)
Country Walks Around the National Forest (Meridian Books 2007)
Walks into History: Cheshire (Countryside 2008)
Historic Walks in and around Newcastle (Carnegie 2008)
Historic Walks in and around Birmingham (Carnegie 2008)

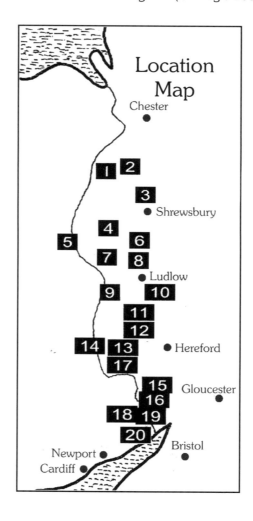

1

A Prehistoric Fort

Old Oswestry

The focal point and most outstanding feature of the route is the massive Iron Age fort of Old Oswestry about a mile (1.6km) to the north of the town centre. There are views of it just after the start and it can be visited near the end. In addition there are extensive views over the Border country and the opportunity to explore the narrow streets and ancient buildings of Oswestry, a most appealing old town.

Distance: 5½ miles/8.9km.
Approximate Time: 3 hours.
Start: Oswestry, Church Street by St Oswald's church, GR SJ288295.
Maps: Explorer 240, Landranger 126.
Car Parking: Pay car parks at Oswestry.
Public Transport: Buses from Shrewsbury, Wrexham, Welshpool, Ellesmere and most of the surrounding towns and villages.
Terrain: Easy walking along tracks and field paths.
Refreshments: Pubs and cafés at Oswestry.

Oswestry's imposing and exceptionally wide church is dedicated to St Oswald, an Anglo-Saxon king of Northumbria and Christian martyr. It is the last of many that have occupied the site for over a thousand years. The tower is the oldest part, dating back to the late eleventh century, but most of the medieval church was so badly damaged in the Civil War that it had to be rebuilt in the 1670s. It fell into ruin again and was comprehensively altered and enlarged during a major restoration by the Victorian architect G.E. Street in the 1870s.

In one corner of the churchyard is an attractive fifteenth century building that was the town's first school, founded in 1407. Now it serves as a visitor and exhibition centre and has a coffee shop.

With your back to the church ❶, turn left along Church Street to where it forks at The Cross. Take the right hand fork and turn left along pedestrianised Bailey Street. Where the street ends, turn left beside the Council Offices and keep ahead below Castle Bank.

Only a few fragments of stonework remain on Castle Bank to remind visitors that this was the site of a powerful medieval fortress that played a leading role in the Welsh Wars. It was so thoroughly dismantled after the Civil War that there is hardly anything left. The site is now a public recreation area and is a fine viewpoint over the town and surrounding area.

Continue along Chapel Street, keep ahead at a crossroads along Oak Street and turn right along York Street. After a right bend, this continues as Liverpool Road. Turn left into Gatacre Road by the left side of a green, bear slightly right at a road junction to continue along Gatacre Avenue and the road ends at a car park. ❷

The right of way continues ahead along an enclosed path but because the first part of it is likely to be overgrown, it is easier to walk along the left edge of the car park and in the corner bear left through a hedge gap to join the enclosed path. Old Oswestry Hill Fort can be seen to the right. After going through a kissing gate, continue along the left edge of a field and where the edge bears left, keep ahead, making for the far right hand corner of the field where you climb a stile.

Bear right across a field to a stile, climb it and continue across the next field.

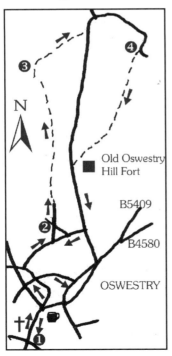

Climb another stile, bear slightly left, head up over the brow of a hill and climb a stile to the right of a gate. From here there are extensive views in front as you head down into a dip, keeping by the right field edge, and then head up to a gate in the far right hand corner. Go through, turn right ❸ along an enclosed track, go through another gate and continue along the left edge of a field. After the next gate there follows a stretch of hedge-lined track and after another gate, the route continues along the right field edge towards a farm. Go through a gate in the corner and continue between the farm buildings to a lane.

Keep ahead to a T-junction, turn right and follow the narrow lane around first a left bend, then a right bend and then another right bend. Where it bends left again, keep ahead along a tarmac track, ❹ passing to the left of farm buildings. Where the track bends right to the farmhouse, keep ahead over a stile and walk along a right field edge. At a hedge corner, keep ahead across the field to a gate, go

Oswestry's medieval church

through and continue along the left edge of the next two fields towards the earthworks of the prehistoric fort.

About 50 yards (46m) before reaching the corner of the second field, bear right across to the base of the fort and continue below it, curving left to emerge onto a lane. Bear left and a kissing gate on the left admits you to the earthworks.

Old Oswestry Hill Fort, built around 3000 years ago, is one of the finest Iron Age forts in Britain. It was occupied from around 800BC to Roman times and the complexity of its ramparts and ditches indicate that there were several stages in its development. It was probably both a defensive stronghold and a civilian settlement. Although it seems to have been abandoned during the Roman occupation, there is no evidence that it was ever besieged and captured by the Romans. At a height of 540 feet (164m), it provides a series of stunning views over the surrounding countryside.

Continue along the lane and at a gap and gate a little further on, a section of Wat's Dyke can be seen to the left running at the base of the fort.

If little is known of Offa's Dyke, the history and purpose of the adjacent Wat's Dyke is even more obscure. The dyke runs for about 40 miles (64km) from Basingwerk Abbey on the Dee estuary to just south of the village of Maesbury, about 2½ miles (4km) south of Oswestry. It is believed to predate Offa's Dyke and was possibly built by Ethelbald of Mercia, Offa's immediate predecessor, in the early eighth century. It runs to the east of Offa's Dyke, roughly parallel and close to it, and may have been an earlier attempt to mark the frontier between the Mercian kingdom and the territories of the Welsh princes before Offa pushed the border further west. Some theories suggest that this dyke was much earlier than the eighth century – possibly Roman or early Anglo-Saxon – but we cannot be certain.

The lane continues into Oswestry. Take the first road on the right (Old Fort Road) which becomes Liverpool Road. Here you rejoin the outward route and retrace your steps to the start.

2

Mellowed Ruins
Whittington Castle and the Llangollen Canal

Starting by the sparse but undeniably picturesque ruins of a medieval castle, the walk takes you across fields and along a quiet lane to the towpath of the Llangollen Canal. After a 1¼ mile (2km) stretch beside the canal, more field paths return you to the start. There are a series of wide and uninterrupted views across the gently undulating landscape of this part of the Welsh Border country that lies between Oswestry and Ellesmere.

Distance: 6½ miles/10.5km
Approximate Time: 3½ hours
Start: Whittington, in front of the castle, GR SJ326312
Maps: Explorer 240, Landranger 126
Car Parking: Pay car park by Whittington Castle
Public Transport: Buses from Shrewsbury, Oswestry and Ellesmere
Terrain: Mainly flat walking along field paths, quiet lane and a canal towpath; some of the field paths may be overgrown and likely to be boggy after rain
Refreshments: Pubs at Whittington, tea room at Whittington Castle, canalside pub at Hindford

---

At first glance the site of Whittington Castle is unusual, low lying and seemingly lacking any of the normal criteria required for the location of a fortress. But when it was built, the surrounding area mainly comprised marshland and water which provided it with some degree of natural defence. The castle was founded in the twelfth century and mainly rebuilt in the early thirteenth century by the Fulkwarine family, its owners for much of the medieval period. Not surprisingly for a castle situated close to the Welsh Border, it was several times the target for Welsh attacks.

From the sixteenth century onwards it declined and became ruinous and during the seventeenth and eighteenth centuries much of its stonework was taken away to be recycled in other buildings. Therefore not much is left apart from the thirteenth century gatehouse, restored in the nineteenth century, but the ruins and their surroundings make a very attractive and nowadays tranquil scene, especially when looking at them from across the moat. Uniquely the castle is now owned and managed by a preservation trust based on the local community.

With your back to the castle ❶, turn right along the main road through the village. After three-quarters of a mile (1.2km) – and just in front of the Babbinswood sign – turn left over a stile and walk across a field to a stile on the far side. Climb it and continue across the next field.

On the far side turn left through a gate, immediately turn right through another gate and walk across a field to a stile at the corner of woodland. After climbing it, continue along a left field edge, by woodland on the left, climb a stile in the corner and keep in the same direction diagonally across the next field. The route continues across an area of rough pasture, which may be overgrown with nettles and difficult to negotiate. Look out for a hedge gap to the right of a solitary tree and after going through it, walk across the next field and go through a gate onto a lane. ❷

Turn left and follow this quiet lane for nearly 1¾ miles (2.8km). Shortly after a left bend by a large house, turn right over a stile at a public footpath sign and bear left across a field, looking out for a stile beside a gate on the far side. After climbing it, turn left ❸ along the A495 – there are verges – and at a public footpath sign, turn right and climb two stiles in quick succession.

Keep along the left edge of a field, cross a footbridge just to the right of the

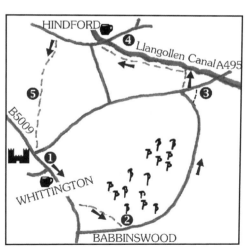

field corner and continue along the left edge of the next field. Look out for a waymarked post where you turn left through a hedge gap and turn right to walk along a right field edge. Head up and climb a stile onto a canal bridge. Do not cross the bridge but bear right to the towpath of the Llangollen Canal and turn left to pass under the bridge.

The Llangollen Canal was a branch of the Shropshire Union Canal and links up with the latter at Hurleston Junction to the north of Nantwich. It was constructed by Thomas Telford in the early nineteenth century and was primarily intended to serve the industrial area around Ruabon in north east Wales. It runs for around 46 miles (74km) across beautiful, largely

Whittington Castle

unspoilt and sometimes dramatic countryside which makes it one of the most popular inland waterways in the country.

Follow the canal to Bridge 11 and immediately after passing under it, turn left and go through a gate onto a lane. ❹ Turn right into Hindford, passing by the Jack Mytton Inn, to a T-junction and turn right again. After almost ½ mile (800m), turn left over a stile, at a public footpath sign, and walk along the right edge of a field. Turn right over a stile, keep along the left edge of the next field, by a wire fence on the left, following the edge as it curves left across rough pasture to reach a footbridge over a stream. Cross it, keep ahead across more rough pasture and cross another footbridge over a stream.

Continue across a rather marshy area, making for a waymarked stile seen ahead. Climb it and head gently uphill across a field, later keeping by its right edge, to a stile in the corner. After climbing it, walk along the left edge of the next field, climb a stile and keep ahead along an enclosed track, descending to a gate. Go through to a T-junction of tracks, turn right through another gate and continue gently uphill. Look out for where you turn left over a stile and descend a steep embankment onto a disused railway track. ❺ Turn right for a few yards and take a path on the left which heads up the opposite embankment to a stile at the top.

Climb it and bear right across a field, making for a waymarked stile in a hedge. After climbing it, continue gently uphill in the same direction across the next field to a gate in the far corner. Go through, keep ahead along a tarmac track to a road and turn right. At a T-junction turn left to return to the start.

3

Grope Lane, Bear Steps and Mardol
Historic Shrewsbury

Shrewsbury is a great place in which to wander and the title of this walk is taken from some of the curious street names to be found in this fascinating old town that possesses a castle, abbey, some impressive churches, a maze of narrow streets and half-hidden alleyways and a wealth of fine buildings. The medieval town was enclosed within a horseshoe bend of the River Severn, protected by a circuit of walls as well as a castle and entered by two bridges, appropriately named English Bridge on the east and Welsh Bridge on the west. Most of these features of interest are included on this route, plus attractive riverside walking and some of the fine parkland for which the town is also noted.

Distance: 3½ miles/5.6km
Approximate Time: 1½ hours
Start: Shrewsbury, The Square, GR SJ492125
Maps: Explorer 241, Landranger 126, or pick up a town map from the tourist information centre
Car Parking: Pay car parks at Shrewsbury
Public Transport: Buses from Oswestry, Welshpool, Telford, Ludlow, Bridgnorth and most surrounding towns and villages; trains from Welshpool, Chester, Wrexham, Hereford, Ludlow and Telford
Terrain: Easy town walking mainly along pavements, cobbled streets and tarmac riverside paths
Refreshments: Plenty of pubs, cafés, restaurants and wine bars at Shrewsbury

---

The walk begins in The Square by the Elizabethan Old Market Hall and the statue to Robert Clive. Clive, who played a major role in the growth of British power in India in the eighteenth century, was a native of Shropshire.

Start by Clive's statue ❶ and with your back to the Old Market Hall, turn right into High Street and almost immediately turn left up Grope Lane, signposted to the Bear Steps. Cross Fish Street and head up the Bear Steps opposite into St Alkmond's Place.

Several medieval towns in England have a street called Grope Lane and the name indicates – in uncompromisingly direct language – that it was the red light district. Interestingly in some places the prudish Victorians tried to cover up the unsavoury origin of these streets by renaming them Grape Lane.

St Alkmond's Place, a picturesque and peaceful spot, is dominated by St Alkmund's church, one of a number of fine churches in Shrewsbury. Of medieval origin, the church was mainly rebuilt in the eighteenth century.

Walk across the churchyard, continue along Church Street to a T-junction and turn left along St Mary's Street, passing St Mary's church.

One of the tallest spires in the country rises above the large and imposing St Mary's church. The building dates from the twelfth century but was enlarged several times over the following centuries. It is particularly noted for the fifteenth century carved wooden ceiling in the nave and an impressive collection of stained glass.

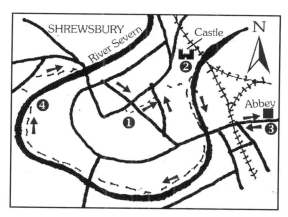

At the next T-junction, turn right into Castle Street and where the road curves slightly left, keep ahead to the castle. ❷

Although it was once one of the greatest and most formidable of Border fortresses, later restoration and demolition has robbed Shrewsbury Castle of much of its medieval grandeur. Nevertheless it is still a fine and interesting building and as it occupies the highest and narrowest part of the peninsula formed by the River Severn, it is inevitably a superb viewpoint.

The first castle was built in the 1070s by the powerful Roger de Montgomery, Earl of Shrewsbury. It was rebuilt and strengthened in the late thirteenth century by Edward I but after Edward's conquest of Wales and the subsequent reduction in warfare on the Welsh Border, the castle declined in importance and saw little further action, apart from during the Civil War. In the late eighteenth century it was remodelled by Thomas Telford as a private house and in 1924 it was acquired by the Corporation of Shrewsbury. It now houses the Shropshire Regimental Museum. Tel: 01743 358 516

Old Market Hall, Shrewsbury

Return to Castle Street, retrace your steps and take the first lane on the left (Windsor Place). Bear left and head quite steeply down St Mary's Water Lane, passing under St Mary's Water Gate to the River Severn.

St Mary's Water Gate, a fragment of the medieval town wall, was the entrance into the town from the river.

Turn right along a riverside path to the English Bridge. In front of it, bear right up steps and turn left over the bridge for a brief detour to the abbey, seen ahead after passing under a railway bridge. **❸**

Most monasteries were located outside the walls of a medieval town and Shrewsbury Abbey is no exception. It was founded as a Benedictine abbey in 1083 by Roger de Montgomery, the same man who built the first castle whose tomb can be seen in the south aisle of the nave. It became one of the wealthiest monasteries in the country and at the time of Henry VIII's dissolution in the 1530s, there were plans to make it the cathedral of a new diocese but these came to nothing. All

Shrewsbury Castle

that survives is the fourteenth century west tower and nave of the church, the latter a fine example of Norman architecture. The present east end – much shorter than the original – is a Victorian rebuilding. Tel: 01743 232 723

Retrace your steps to the riverside path and continue along it, following the river around a right bend. Just beyond a footbridge you can see over to the right the only remaining stretch of Shrewsbury's medieval walls. Later after passing the next bridge, St Chad's church is seen over to the right, well worth a short diversion across the park.

After the old St Chad's church fell into disrepair, a new one was built in the late eighteenth century on a different site. It is an impressive and striking Georgian building with a circular nave, one of the largest in the country.

Turn left over the next footbridge (Porthill Bridge), ❹ turn right along a road and take the first lane on the right (Water Lane) to return to the Severn. Turn left along the riverside path to the Welsh Bridge and immediately after passing under it, turn sharp left to the road.

Turn left to cross the bridge, follow the road to the left and turn right up Mardol, another of Shrewsbury's picturesque streets, to a T-junction. Cross the road and take the alley in front – to the right of the National Westminster Bank – which leads back into The Square.

4

Spectacular Rocky Outcrops
Stiperstones

In some ways this walk is more reminiscent of some of the lonelier and more remote parts of Dartmoor or the Pennines than Shropshire. It takes you across an area of wild, heathery and lonely moorland and the highlight is the walk along part of the Stiperstones ridge, passing some of the large and spectacular outcrops of rock which are its main features. An additional bonus is stunning views over the Border country.

Distance: 4 miles/6.4km
Approximate Time: 2 hours
Start: The Bog car park, from the A488 at Ploxgreen take the lane to Snailbeach and Stiperstones and The Bog (clearly signposted) is about two miles (3.2km) beyond Stiperstones village, GR SO356979
Maps: Explorer 216, Landranger 126
Car Parking: The Bog
Public Transport: The Stiperstones Shuttle bus, part of the Shropshire Hills Shuttles, runs from Easter to the end of October. It links the villages that surround Stiperstones and stops at The Bog. For details phone 01588 673888 or contact the local tourist information centre.
Terrain: Mainly on clear tracks at the beginning and end and a rocky path along the ridge, some modest climbing
Refreshments: Light refreshments at The Bog Visitor Centre (open from Easter to the end of October)

In Victorian times The Bog was a lead mining community of around 200 people with cottages, school, pub and a miner's institute. The mine closed down in 1883, the people drifted away and most of the surviving buildings were demolished in 1972. Little is now left apart from some of the remains of the mine itself and the former school house, now a Visitor Centre, which is open between Easter and the end of October. Tel: 01743 792 484.

Turn right out of the car park ❶ along the lane. Follow it around a left bend, head uphill and at a sharp right bend, keep ahead over a stile. As you continue uphill along an enclosed track, some of the rocky outcrops

The Devil's Chair

on the Stiperstones ridge can be seen ahead. At the top of the rise, go through a gate (or climb a stile) to enter the Stiperstones National Nature Reserve.

The somewhat forbidding and mysterious looking five mile (8km) long ridge of the Stiperstones is a conspicuous landmark above the surrounding countryside of Shropshire and the Welsh Border country. What gives the ridge its distinctive appearance is the series of jagged outcrops that punctuate it at intervals. These are the remnants of quartzite rocks formed around 480 million years ago. During the Ice Age the surrounding softer rocks were eroded and the quartzite outcrops were subjected to constant freezing and thawing, hence their shattered and jagged appearance. The air of mystery and menace that surrounds them has made the rocks the setting of numerous myths and legends.

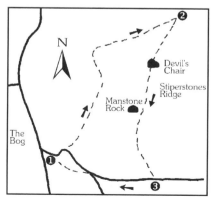

Continue along the track, negotiating a series of gate/stile combinations, to reach a crossways. Turn right and head uphill towards the ridge, passing the boundary fence of Pennerley Reservoir, climbing steadily to another crossways at the top. ❷ To the left is Shepherds Rock but the route continues to the right along a rocky path to the Devil's Chair, the most prominent of the series of outcrops on the ridge.

The next part of the route is the most spectacular as you continue past the Devil's Chair to the Manstone Rock. At 1759 feet (536m), this is the highest point on the ridge and is topped by a trig point. Passing to the left of the rock, keep ahead to the next outcrop, Cranberry Rock. After keeping to the left of this, the path starts to descend, bears left off the ridge and becomes a broad grassy path. At the bottom go through a gate into a car park and turn right to a T-junction. ❸

Turn right along a narrow lane, at the next T-junction turn right again and after about 50 yards (46m), turn left over a stile at a Shropshire Way sign. Turn half-right and walk across a field to the right hand one of two waymarked stiles seen ahead. After climbing it, keep ahead downhill across a field – The Bog Visitor Centre can be seen ahead – following a line of telegraph posts and keeping to the right of a hedgeline to reach a kissing gate. Go through, descend steps and walk along an enclosed winding path between trees and bracken which emerges into The Bog car park.

5

Border Fortresses
Around Montgomery

The Severn valley around Montgomery has always been a major routeway and its great strategic importance is clearly obvious from the number of fortified sites, which range from an Iron Age fort to a thirteenth century castle. The route passes two of these defences and you are able to see a third one from a distance. This is also a walk of magnificent views throughout, especially from the prominent war memorial on Town Hill overlooking the valley.

Distance: 3½ miles/5.6km
Approximate Time: 2 hours
Start: Montgomery, Broad Street in front of the Town Hall, GR SO223965
Maps: Explorer 216; Landranger 137
Car Parking: Parking spaces in the centre of Montgomery
Public Transport: Buses from Welshpool, Newtown and Shrewsbury
Terrain: Clear paths, one steep climb through woodland
Refreshments: Pubs and cafés at Montgomery

S tart in Broad Street ❶ and facing the Georgian Town Hall, turn right along Arthur Street, passing the Old Bell, formerly an inn and now a Local History Centre. Descend to a junction, turn left and the road curves left below the steep wooded hill which is topped by the ruins of Montgomery Castle.

Ignore the first public footpath sign on the left but at the second one (where the road curves slightly right), turn left over a stile, turn right and follow a path uphill across a field into woodland. As the path curves left and continues more steeply up through the trees, there is a superb view to the right over the Severn valley, with the wooded mound of Hen Domen clearly seen below.

Hen Domen is Montgomery's first castle, founded by the powerful Norman baron Roger de Montgomery, Earl of Shrewsbury, in the 1070s. The name Montgomery comes from the area in Normandy from where he came. It was a motte and bailey castle and comprised a motte or mound and a bailey or courtyard with timber buildings. The motte and the earthworks of the bailey survive. In 1102 the castle was

View over the Severn Vally near Montgomery

forfeited to the Crown following a rebellion by Robert de Montgomery and in 1223 it was abandoned and superseded by the present castle.

Continue up to the top of Fridd Faldwyn where you emerge from the trees and continue across the site of a prehistoric fort, the earliest of the various defensive structures in the Montgomery area.

It is difficult to make out many of the earthworks of the Iron Age fort on Ffridd Faldwyn, except on the south side after you start to descend where the banks and ditches are much more obvious. The fort was built around 500BC on the site of an earlier Neolithic settlement and has a superb location, 814 feet (248m) above the path descends gently and passes thrhe Severn valley.

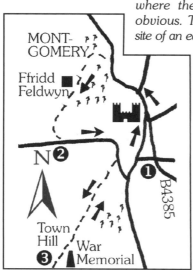

Tough the outer defences of the fort to a stile. Climb it, descend a steep embankment in front and keep ahead across a field. In front the war memorial on top of Town Hill can be seen and to the left the ruins of Montgomery Castle come into view. Climb a stile onto a lane ❷ and turn left to where the lane bends right by the castle entrance. In order to visit the

ruins, walk through the car park and turn left along a path.

The fairly sparse but nevertheless impressive remains of Montgomery Castle occupy a long, steep, narrow ridge above the town with commanding views over the Severn valley, one of the key routeways in the Border country. It was built in 1223 by Henry III during his campaigns against the powerful Welsh prince Llywelyn the Great and replaced the earlier motte and bailey castle at Hen Domen about 1¼ miles (2km) to the north west.

In its early years the castle withstood several attacks by Llywelyn and his son David but after Edward I's conquest of Wales in the late thirteenth century and the onset of greater peace and stability in the area, its strategic importance declined. Despite neglect and deterioration, its buildings were patched up several times and the castle last saw action in the Civil War when it was captured by the Parliamentarians. It was demolished soon afterwards.

Where the lane bends right by the entrance to the castle, turn right through a kissing gate, at a footpath sign to War Memorial, and head uphill along a wooded path. On meeting a track, bear left along it and continue steadily up through the trees to reach a waymarked post. At this point bear right off the path and walk up to the Montgomeryshire County War Memorial. ❸

The memorial commemorates the men of Montgomeryshire who gave their lives in the First and Second World Wars. It stands at a height of 1050 feet (320m) and adjoining it are a trig point and viewfinder. The 360 degree views from here over the Border country are magnificent and the viewfinder enables you to identify the individual landmarks.

Retrace your steps to the lane, follow it around the right bend but immediately take the narrow lane to the left of it. This heads steeply downhill back into the town to return you to the start.

The remains of Montgomery Castle

6

Steep Valleys and Extensive Views
The Long Mynd

This is one of the great classic walks of the Welsh Border country. The first part of the route is a climb – steep and rocky at times – through the beautiful Carding Mill Valley onto the broad and open ridge of the Long Mynd. From here you head steadily up to its highest point at Pole Bank, a magnificent viewpoint. The descent into Little Stretton is mainly along clear grassy paths, with more outstanding views, and the final leg is through woodland and along a road.

Distance: 8 miles/12.9km.
Approximate time: 4 hours.
Start: Church Stretton, The Square, GR SO453937.
Maps: Explorer 217, Landranger 137 .
Car Parking: Pay car park at Church Stretton.
Public Transport: Buses from Shrewsbury and Ludlow; trains from Shrewsbury, Ludlow and Hereford.
Terrain: Mixture of rocky and grassy paths by streams, through woodland and across moorland; some steep ascents and descents.
Refreshments: Pubs and cafes at Church Stretton, National Trust café in the Carding Mill Valley, pub at Little Stretton.

Because of the Alpine appearance of the local terrain, the Victorians called the area around Church Stretton 'little Switzerland' and in the nineteenth century the town became a health resort. It retains a pleasantly old fashioned air and makes an excellent walking centre, situated in the Onny valley, surrounded by hills and moorland, at the hub of an extensive network of public footpaths and well endowed with hotels, guest houses, pubs and cafes. Most of the town was destroyed by a great fire in 1593 but one building that survived is the church which dates back to Norman times.

Start by walking northwards along High Street ❶ and at a crossroads, turn left along Burway Road. The lane curves right, heads uphill and just after crossing a cattle grid, bear right onto a track which narrows to a path and descends to a tarmac track. Continue gently uphill through the

Carding Mill Valley, passing the Chalet Pavilion which houses a National Trust information centre, shop and café.

The beauty and accessibility of the Carding Mill Valley makes it an extremely popular spot on fine weekends and bank holidays. It gets its name from a carding mill that was located here until it closed down in the early years of the twentieth century. The carding process was when wool was 'carded' or combed before being spun into yarn.

Where the tarmac track ends at a parking area, keep ahead along a path. At a fork immediately after fording a stream, ❷ take the left hand path – here leaving the main valley – initially climbing some rock-hewn steps and continuing along a rocky path up the ever narrowing valley. In front of the Light Spout waterfall, turn right to ascend steps and continue up to the head of the valley.

Where the path curves right, look out for a waymarked post where you turn sharp left, walk past another waymarked post and bear right, climbing between bracken, to emerge onto the open, heathery moorland of the Long Mynd. The grassy path curves first left, then bears right and heads across to a

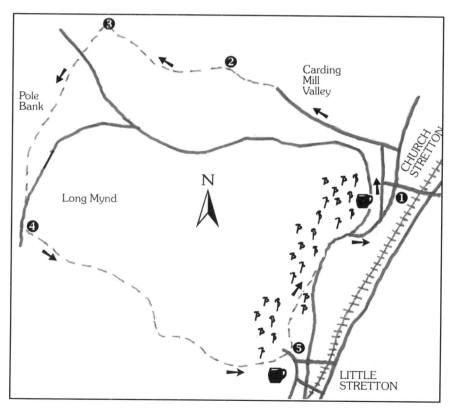

The Carding Mill Valley

junction of tracks. **❸** Cross the first track, bear left along the second one – at a blue-waymarked post – and follow the track to a lane and parking area called the Shooting Box. Cross the lane and keep ahead, climbing steadily to the trig point and viewfinder at Pole Bank.

At 1693 feet (516m), Pole Bank is the highest point on the broad, whale-backed hill of the Long Mynd which rises abruptly above the western side of the Onny valley. To the east it overlooks Wenlock Edge, Caer Caradoc and Ragleth Hill and to the west the hills of the Border country. 'Mynd' is the Welsh word for mountain, hence Long Mynd literally means long mountain. Its eastern slopes are cut into by a number of narrow, steep-sided valleys or hollows, called batches, which provide the main access to the summit for walkers.

The all round views are magnificent and the viewfinder at Pole Bank conveniently indicates the well-known landmarks that can be seen from here if you are fortunate enough to get a fine day. These include all the Shropshire hills and in exceptionally clear conditions can extend far into Wales to Cadair Idris, the Brecon Beacons and even Snowdon.

Continue past the trig point to a lane and turn right. This part of the lane is on the line of a prehistoric route called The Portway. After just over ¼ mile (0.4km) and just before the lane curves slightly right, turn left **❹** onto a clear grassy track across the open moor. At a fork take the left hand path which continues over the shoulder of a hill and descends into a dip called Barrister's Plain. From here there are grand views to the left over the steep-sided valley of Ashes Hollow. The path rises again and then descends first along the left side of Callow Hollow and then along the right side of Small Batch. Later it descends more steeply – first by a fence on the right and then above a stream on the left – to a gate. Go through, keep ahead along a tree-shaded path,

passing a cottage, cross a footbridge over a stream and turn right onto a lane.
5 Continue along the lane if you wish to make a short detour into Little Stretton, for the pub and church.

The hamlet of Little Stretton has an unusual thatched, black and white wooden church, erected in 1903.

In order to continue the walk, immediately turn left over a stile and head up an enclosed path which bends left and keeps above the valley. Later walk along the top edge of steeply sloping woodland to a stile. Climb it, keep ahead to a fingerpost and bear right across a field, drawing closer to its right edge and continuing alongside it. Head downhill through trees to climb a stile and continue down, bending right to emerge onto a road. Turn left and follow the road for three-quarters of a mile(1.2km) back to the start at Church Stretton.

7

Quietest Place under the Sun
Clun Valley

In 'The Shropshire Lad', A.E. Housman wrote: 'Clunton and Clunbury, Clungunford and Clun, are the quietest places under the sun'. Although written in 1896, this peaceful walk confirms that these words still hold true today. It is a flat walk through the valley of the River Clun between Clun and the hamlet of Witcott Keysett. At the approximate half-way point, a modest climb brings you onto a 850 foot (259m) ridge from where the views over the valley are superb, with both the castle and church at Clun visible on the horizon.

Distance: 5 miles/8km.
Approximate time: 2½ hours.
Start: Clun, The Square, GR SO301809.
Maps: Explorer 201, Landranger 137.
Car Parking: Pay car parks at Clun.
Public Transport: Buses from Ludlow, Bishop's Castle, Knighton and Craven Arms.
Terrain: Flat and easy valley walking with one modest climb and descent, note there are approximately 27 stiles.
Refreshments: Pubs and cafés at Clun.

Clun has an off the beaten track feel about it and is one of those places where it is difficult to know whether to describe it as a large village or a small town. In size it is little more than a village but it has the appearance of a town with an eighteenth century former town hall, now a museum, in the Square. It was once a thriving woollen centre with more shops and pubs and a larger population than now.

The ruins of Clun Castle occupy a knoll above the town and river. It was founded by the Normans around 1100 as a simple wooden motte and bailey structure and was later rebuilt in stone. The 80 foot (25m) high twelfth century keep is unusual in that it was built into the side of the motte or mound instead of on the top. The castle was besieged several times by the Welsh, the last occasion being in the early fifteenth century during Owain Glyndwr's revolt. By this time the castle had already deteriorated as its owners, the Fitzalan family, had abandoned

Clun for the more spacious and settled environment of their principal residence at Arundel in Sussex.

Across the medieval bridge on the south side of the town stands the Norman church, heavily restored in the Victorian period. In the churchyard is the tomb of the playwright John Osborne, author of Look Back in Anger and one of the 'angry young men' of the 1950s.

Starting in The Square ❶ with your back to the White Horse, turn right and first right again, in the Bishop's Castle and Shrewsbury direction. At a public footpath sign and sign to Clun Castle, turn left along an enclosed track – here joining the Shropshire Way – and in front of the gate to the castle, turn right over a stile.

Head downhill below the castle ruins to a stile. Climb it, continue along a track in front of a row of houses and where the track ends, keep ahead along an enclosed path. Turn left over a footbridge, turn right along an enclosed path, climb a stile and continue across a field, keeping parallel to the right edge. Cross another footbridge, climb a stile, walk along the right edge of the next field and look out for a yellow waymark which directs you to turn right over a stile. Turn left to continue by the little River Unk, climb a stile, keep ahead along a partially enclosed path and after climbing two stiles in quick succession, continue along an enclosed path, climbing two more stiles to emerge onto a lane. ❷

Turn left and after 300 yards (274m), look out for a public footpath sign on the left where you go

through a gate. Walk along a right field edge over a low brow and continue down to a gate in the corner. Go through, keep ahead along an enclosed track, go through another gate and continue down to the River Clun where there is a ford and a footbridge. Do not cross the footbridge but turn right through a gate and walk across a meadow, making for a gate in the far right corner. Go through, continue by the river, climb a stile and turn right to climb another one. Bear left and head gently uphill across the middle of the field, looking out for a stile on the far side about 100 yards (91m) before the corner.

Climb it and turn left along a lane. After three-quarters of a mile (1.2km) and just before reaching the first of the houses in the hamlet of Witcott Keysett, turn right along a hedge-and tree-lined track. ❸ Head steadily uphill, go through a gate, keep ahead and immediately after climbing another gate, turn right over a stile, here rejoining the Shropshire Way for the remainder of the walk. Keep along a right field edge, climb a stile and continue across two fields. From the

Clun Castle

broad ridge, there are superb views all around and Clun Castle can be seen ahead in the distance. Head towards the right edge of the second field, continue downhill along it and just before reaching the corner, look out for a half-hidden stile in the hedge on the right.

Climb it, pass through a hedge gap and continue downhill along the right edge of the next field. In the bottom corner climb a stile onto a lane, cross over and climb the stile opposite. ❷ Walk along an enclosed path, here picking up the outward route and retrace your steps to the start.

Some countryside near Clun

8

A Picturesque Medieval Manor House
Stoke Wood and Stokesay Castle

From Craven Arms the route takes you across fields and along the edge of woodlands to the south west of the town. The scenic highlight is the descent across fields on emerging from Stoke Wood, from where you enjoy grand views of Stokesay Castle against a backcloth of wooded hills.

Distance: 4½ miles/7.2km.
Approximate Time: 2½ hours.
Start: Craven Arms, road junction in town centre by the Craven Arms Hotel, GR SO434828. Alternatively start at the Shropshire Hills Discovery Centre just to the south of the town centre.
Maps: Explorer 217; Landranger 137.
Car Parking: Pay car park at Craven Arms or free parking at the Shropshire Hills Discovery Centre.
Public Transport: Buses from Shrewsbury and Ludlow, trains from Shrewsbury, Ludlow, Hereford and Knighton.
Terrain: Gently undulating route mainly on well-waymarked field and woodland paths.
Refreshments: Pubs and cafés at Craven Arms, café at Shropshire Hills Discovery Centre, tea room at Stokesay Castle.

Craven Arms takes its name from a hotel and is a mainly nineteenth century creation when it became a rail junction. Here the Heart of Wales line branches off from the north-south line between Shrewsbury, Ludlow and Hereford. Although a somewhat undistinguished town, it has a fine location in the valley of the little River Onny between Wenlock Edge and the Long Mynd and makes a good walking centre. Appropriately its main attraction is the Shropshire Hills Discovery Centre, housed in a new and imaginative grass-roofed building which contains information on the archaeology, history and geology of the surrounding hills. Tel: 01588 676060

Start at the crossroads in the town centre ❶ and facing the Craven Arms, turn left along the A49, in the Leominster and Ludlow direction. At a public footpath sign 'Wart Hill Wander' opposite the Shropshire Hills Discovery Centre, turn right onto a tarmac path. Continue along the road ahead and where it ends, keep ahead along a hedge-and tree-lined track.

Pass under a railway bridge, continue along the track and just after climbing a stile, bear left and head gently uphill along the left edge of a field. Climb a stile at a fingerpost, ❷ keep straight ahead across the next field and on the far side, continue through a belt of trees to a gate. Go through, turn right and head uphill along the right edge of the field.

After curving left, continue along the right edge of a series of fields, negotiating a succession of gates and stiles – to the right is Sallow Coppice – finally reaching a track by a farm and lane. ❸ Turn left along the track and at a junction of paths and tracks on the edge of woodland – where the track forks – take the left hand track to continue through the mainly coniferous plantation of Stoke Wood.

After about half a mile (0.8km), look out for a waymarked post where you bear left to a stile. Climb it and as you head downhill across three fields and over three stiles, there are superb views ahead of Stokesay Castle. Go through a gate at the bottom end of the last field, walk along a tree-lined track, carefully cross a railway line, keep ahead and go through a gate onto a lane. Turn left to Stokesay Castle and church.

Both when approaching it and viewing it close up, Stokesay Castle is undeniably picturesque. It is not a castle but a fortified thirteenth cen-

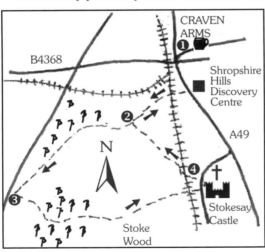

tury manor house and was built by Lawrence of Ludlow, a wealthy local wool merchant, who purchased the site in 1281. Although it was fortified, with a free standing tower – the equivalent of a keep – on the south side, outer walls and a moat, it was built more for comfort than defence and it is doubtful how far its defences could have withstood a prolonged siege. Perhaps they were built more as a gesture or status symbol and not intended to be taken too seriously. There is no doubt that the Welsh Border country was still dangerous and lawless but the construction of Stokesay coincided with the conquest of Wales by Edward I, which is just the time when the area started to become more peaceful. The manor house mainly comprises a large hall with two towers at either end. The half-timbered gatehouse was built later in the early seventeenth century to replace an earlier one. Although Stokesay saw some action in the Civil War, there was little destruction either during or after that conflict apart from the demolition of the outer walls. Tel: 01588 672544

The adjacent church was originally built in the twelfth century but it was badly damaged during the Civil War when it was attacked by a Parliamentary army because Royalist troops had taken refuge inside. It was rebuilt in the 1650s, a rare example of a church dating from the Cromwellian era.

Just before reaching the castle, the route continues through a gate on the left at a Shropshire Way sign. ❹ Walk along a track by a pool on the left, go under a railway bridge and turn right along a right field edge. Turn left to continue by a hedgeline on the right to a stile. Climb it, head gently uphill along a right field edge and at a fingerpost, turn right over a stile. (2) Here you rejoin the outward route and retrace your steps to the start.

Stokesay Castle

9

Along Offa's Dyke

Knighton and the Teme Valley

This walk enables you to see and walk beside some of the most impressive surviving stretches of Offa's Dyke. An easy opening ramble by the River Teme is followed by a short but steep ascent onto a ridge. Then comes a glorious 1¼ mile (2.8km) walk beside Offa's Dyke during which you can enjoy and appreciate not only the unique interest of the dyke itself but also the outstanding views over the Teme valley and surrounding hills. A fairly steep descent brings you to a narrow, quiet lane which leads back to the start.

Distance: 5½ miles/8.9km.
Approximate time: 3 hours.
Start: Knighton, by the Clock Tower, GR SO286724.
Maps: Explorer 201, Landranger 137.
Car Parking: Pay car parks at Knighton.
Public Transport: Buses from Ludlow, Clun and Kington; trains from Craven Arms and Llandrindod Wells.
Terrain: Steep climb, followed by an easy ridge walk and a steep descent; well-waymarked paths throughout.
Refreshments: Pubs and cafés at Knighton.

Knighton is the ultimate Border town, situated right on the line of the English-Welsh border though predominantly in Wales, apart from the railway station. It also stands at the approximate half-way point on Offa's Dyke Path and its Welsh name, Tref-y-Clawdd, means 'the town on the dyke'. The Offa's Dyke Centre is passed near both the start and finish of the walk and a visit here is well worthwhile, with displays on the history and building of the dyke and books, leaflets and information both on the dyke itself and Offa's Dyke Path National Trail. Tel: 01547 528753

Start in the town centre by the Victorian Clock Tower **❶** and walk along West Street, in the direction of Offa's Dyke Centre. On reaching the Centre, bear right onto a tarmac path which curves right and at an Offa's Dyke Path sign where the path ends, keep ahead across the grass and descend steps.

Keep ahead through trees, continue across another grassy area and then through more trees to the River Teme and turn left onto a tree-shaded riverside path. After going through two kissing gates, walk along an enclosed path, go through another kissing gate and continue across a meadow, following the river around a right curve. Go through a gate, turn right to cross a footbridge over the Teme and turn left to cross a railway line. Go through another gate and continue by the river to a fingerpost where you turn right and head up to go through a gate onto a lane. ❷

Cross over, go through a gate opposite and head uphill along a path between embankments. The path bends right and continues steeply up through woodland to a T-junction. Turn left, continue uphill and at a fork by an Offa's Dyke Path post, take the right hand path. Now comes the steepest part of the climb to the next footpath post where you turn left and continue climbing more gently along a ridge. The route continues through a series of gates mainly following the base of Offa's Dyke, which can be clearly seen most of the time. To the left are superb views over the Teme valley.

Offa's Dyke, Britain's longest archaeological monument, is a remarkable feat of construction although very little is known about it. It is thought to have been built in the late eighth century by Offa the Great of Mercia, the most powerful Anglo-Saxon king of the time. What its exact purpose was remains unclear. The main theories are that it was either a defensive structure, or a boundary marker between Mercia and the territories of the Welsh princes, or perhaps both. For most of its length it consisted of a rampart up to 25 feet (8m) high with a ditch on the western side. The line of the dyke has been traced for most of its length – 80 miles (129km) – from Chepstow to near Wrexham but no evidence of any wooden buildings or any kind of fortifications that may have been linked with it have ever been found. Much of it has inevitably been obliterated over the centuries – in fact it is a miracle that any has survived at all – but some of its best preserved sections can be seen both to the north and south of Knighton.

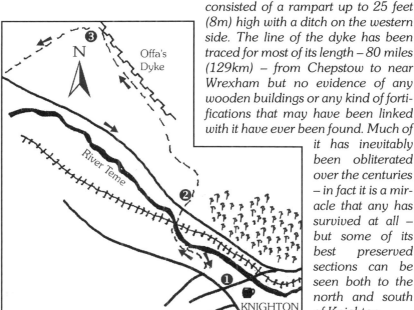

The River Teme near Knighton

Offa's Dyke Path is one of Britain's most popular National Trails. It runs through the Border country for 177 miles (285km) from the Severn estuary near Chepstow to Prestatyn on the North Wales coast. It follows the ancient dyke as far as possible – for about 30 miles (55km) – and elsewhere the line of the path has been chosen for its scenic qualities.

After going through a gate to reach a crossways and fingerpost, turn left off Offa's Dyke Path ❸ and head steeply downhill along a track. Cross a track, go through a gate by a cottage and continue less steeply down an enclosed track which bends left to a lane. Turn left, in the Knighton direction, and after 1½ miles (2.4km), turn right through a gate at an Offa's Dyke Path post. ❷ Here you rejoin the outward route and retrace your steps to the start.

A stretch of Offa's Dyke above the Teme Valley

10

Where the Course of English History was Changed

Ludlow and Mortimer Forest

After an opening stretch across fields, most of the rest of the route is through woodland, first the conifer woodlands of Mortimer Forest which lie to the south west of Ludlow and later the beautiful deciduous woodlands that clothe the steep slopes of Whitcliffe Common. On the latter stages of the walk there are magnificent views over the town and castle of Ludlow and the surrounding countryside.

Distance: 5 miles/8km.
Approximate Time: 2½ hours.
Start: Ludlow, Castle Square, GR SO510746.
Maps: Explorer 203, Landranger 137 .
Car Parking: Plenty of pay car parks in Ludlow town centre.
Public Transport: Buses from Shrewsbury, Kidderminster, Hereford, Bridgnorth and most of the surrounding towns; trains from Shrewsbury and Hereford.
Terrain: Modest climbing mainly along clear and well signed field and woodland paths and tracks.
Refreshments: Pubs, cafés and coffee shops at Ludlow.

By any standards the hilltop town of Ludlow ranks as one of the most attractive and unspoilt old towns in England. Its streets, lined by handsome half-timbered and Georgian buildings, descend steeply from the medieval church and castle to the banks of the River Teme.

Castle and church dominate the town's skyline. Ludlow Castle occupies a commanding position on a cliff overlooking the river and is one of the finest and most complete of the surviving Border castles. It was begun in the late eleventh century soon after the Norman Conquest and retains its Norman keep and a rare example of a twelfth century circular chapel. In the fourteenth century it came into the possession of the powerful Roger Mortimer, Earl of March. He and his successors considerably enlarged the castle and after the accession of Edward IV – who was related to the Mortimers – in 1461, it became a royal fortress.

Two events at the castle can be said to have had a profound effect on the course of English history. The first of these concerns the two young sons of Edward IV, the future Edward V and his brother Richard Duke of York. They lived here from 1472 until their father's death in 1483 when they travelled to the capital for Edward V's coronation. This never happened because the throne was seized by their uncle, Richard of Gloucester, and the two young princes were imprisoned and subsequently murdered in the Tower of London. This ushered in the short-lived reign of Richard III, ended by his death at the battle of Bosworth in 1485 and the accession of Henry VII, the first of the Tudors. The second event revolves around Arthur Prince of Wales, Henry VII's eldest son and first husband of Catherine of Aragon. He and his wife were at Ludlow when he died prematurely in 1502. This led to the eventual succession of his younger brother, the future Henry VIII,

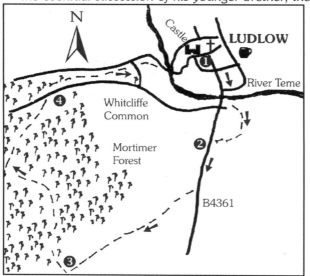

with all the religious and political upheavals that his reign entailed.

Ludlow Castle was at its height during the Tudor period when it became the headquarters of the Lord President of the Council of Wales. At this time the north gatehouse was built and the castle was further altered and enlarged to make it a more comfortable and palatial residence. Although it suffered little damage during the Civil War, it was dismantled soon afterwards and subsequently fell into ruin. Tel: 01584873355

Rivalling the castle is the superb cruciform church, approached through a maze of narrow streets and alleys. It is a fine example of a prosperous town church, with a lofty central tower, 138 feet (42m) high, and an interior of cathedral-like proportions. First built in the eleventh century, it was rebuilt in the early thirteenth century and enlarged in the fifteenth century from the profits of the wool trade. A.E. Housman, author of A Shropshire Lad is buried in the churchyard.

With your back to the castle ❶, walk along High Street (or any of the parallel narrow streets or alleys) towards the church and in front of the eighteenth century Buttercross, turn right down Broad Street. Pass under Broad Gate, one of the gateways in the medieval walls that encircled Ludlow, continue down to the River Teme and cross Ludford Bridge.

Immediately turn left along Park Road and follow it around a right bend. Where the road peters out, keep ahead through a small parking area, go through a kissing gate and continue along a grassy path by a wall bordering woodland on the right. On reaching a tarmac track, turn right through a gate and walk along a track, passing in front of houses, to rejoin the road. ❷

Turn left and after just over a quarter of a mile (400m), look out for a public footpath sign on the left. Although the sign is on the left hand side of the road, you turn right along a drive and after passing to the right of a house, continue along an enclosed path to a stile. Climb it, walk first along a right field edge and then an enclosed track and at a waymarked post, turn right onto another track. Almost immediately bear left onto a narrower path between tree-lined embankments and continue to a gate. Go through and keep along the left edge of a field.

Climbing gently all the while, pass to the left of a house, continue along an enclosed track and go through a gate to enter the conifer woodlands of Mortimer Forest. ❸

The area now covered by Mortimer Forest occupies part of the ancient forests of Bringewood, Monktree and Deerfold. Later these hunting

Dinham Bridge

grounds became part of the vast estates of the powerful Mortimers, the Marcher Lords, hence the name of the present forest. It mainly comprises conifer woodlands first planted by the Forestry Commission in the 1920s.

At a U-bend, take the right hand track which climbs steadily along the right inside edge of the trees to reach a three-way junction. Keep ahead along the middle path (signed Climbing Jack and Whitcliffe Loop) and continue through the trees, following the regular Forestry Commission waymarks to a crossways. Turn left along a track, head uphill to a T-junction and turn right onto a broad track.

Head gently downhill to Whitcliffe car park and continue down to a road. ❹ Cross over to a Mortimer Trail fingerpost and take a downhill path through woodland. Look out for the next waymarked post where you turn sharp right and continue down through this beautiful woodland, later keeping parallel to a road below and eventually emerging onto that road.

Turn right and at a fork immediately in front take the right hand upper road. At a sign for Whitcliffe Common, the route turns left onto a path but a brief detour ahead leads to a parking area beside the road and a magnificent view over Ludlow. There are a number of paths from here that descend to Dinham Bridge but some are steep and potentially slippery and it is best to return to the Whitcliffe Common sign where the main path leads off from the

Looking across to Ludlow Castle

Photo: Peter Groves

road. Head down it, via steps in places, through more woodland, eventually bending left and descending to a road at Dinham Bridge.

The 52 acres that make up Whitcliffe Common are but a fragment of the medieval common on which the burgesses of Ludlow had the right to graze livestock, quarry stone and gather firewood. From the higher points the views over Ludlow, the River Teme and the Border country are superb.

After crossing the bridge, head uphill and follow the road to the left, keeping by the line of the castle walls to return to Castle Square.

The River Teme near Ludlow

11

Castle, Church and Iron Age Fort
Croft Castle and Croft Ambrey Fort

The walk starts near Croft Castle and the adjoining church and climbs gently through a wooded valley up to the ridge occupied by the Iron Age fort of Croft Ambrey, a superb viewpoint. The return leg is an equally gentle descent, again chiefly through woodland with a final short stretch across parkland.

Distance: 3½ miles/5.6km
Approximate Time: 2 hours
Start: Croft Castle, GR 452656
Maps: Explorer 203, Landranger 137
Car Parking: National Trust car park at Croft Castle
Public Transport: None
Terrain: Easy ascent and descent along good paths mainly through woodland
Refreshments: Tea room at Croft Castle

Croft Castle is basically a late medieval fortified manor house, later rebuilt as a Gothic-style mansion. It has been the home of the Croft family since the 11th century, apart from a gap of nearly 200 years when it was sold in 1746 because of financial difficulties. The family repurchased it in 1923 and still live here but the castle is now maintained by the National Trust. The present building, on the site of an earlier Norman castle, dates mainly from the fifteenth century but was extensively remodelled in the eighteenth century, to convert it into a more comfortable home. It is noted for its plasterwork ceilings and fine furniture. There is a walled garden and the castle is surrounded by extensive parkland. Tel: 01568 780246

From the car park ❶ walk back along the drive and immediately after going through a gate beside a cattle grid, turn left onto a path through woodland. The path curves gradually left, descends and keeps along the side of the Fishpool valley.

After ascending and meeting another track, continue through the wooded valley, following the regular public footpath signs and later ascending again. Keep on the main path all the while, passing two pools, to reach a T-junction.

Croft Castle

Turn left, head more steeply uphill, keep ahead at a crossways, cross another track and continue up to a gate at the top. **2**

Go through, turn left at a T-junction and a stile on the left admits you to Croft Ambrey Fort. Follow a grassy path up to the summit of the fort.

The well preserved ramparts and ditches of Croft Ambrey occupy a roughly triangular shaped area of around 32 acres and the extensive views from here over the Border country are magnificent. This Iron Age hill fort appears to have been continuously occupied from the sixth century BC to AD48 after which it was abandoned.

At a fork, take the left hand grassy path heading gently downhill. After descending the outer ramparts of the fort, the path bends left and continues down to a stile. Climb it and turn left along a path which heads down through woodland to a path junction. **3** Do not take the yellow-waymarked public footpath but climb a stile to the left of it to continue along a blue-waymarked track, signed 'Forestry Commission, Croft Castle'. Head down through a conifer plantation, keep ahead at a crossways and continue down to a kissing gate on the edge of the trees where the track bends left.

After going through the gate, almost immediately bear left onto a path through a group of huge and gnarled old trees to a

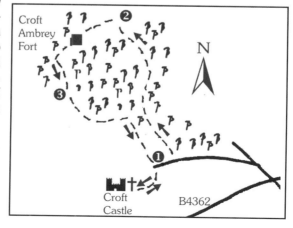

stile. Climb it and continue downhill along a path which keeps by the right in-side edge of woodland to a gate and stile. Go through the gate and keep ahead across open grassland, making for a kissing gate beside a cattle grid.

The car park is just ahead but in order to visit the church, walk along the tarmac drive in front, passing the entrance to the castle, and go through a kissing gate. Keep ahead and when you see a gate and stile over to the right, walk across the grass to them. Do not climb the stile but go through a metal kissing gate on the right and continue across the grass to the church.

At Croft, as at many English country houses, castle and church stand side by side. The attractive little thirteenth century church contains the tomb of Sir Richard Croft, one of the most illustrious members of the family, who played a major role in the Wars of the Roses.

From the church retrace your steps to the car park.

The church beside Croft Castle

12

By the River Arrow
Eardisland and Pembridge

The route takes in two of Herefordshire's most attractive black and white villages. The opening stretch between Eardisland and Pembridge is along a quiet lane and across fields on the north side of the River Arrow. After a brief detour into Pembridge, the return leg is across a succession of delightful meadows on the south side of the river.

Distance: 5 miles/8km.
Approximate Time: 2½ hours.
Start: Eardisland car park, GR 420586.
Maps: Explorers 201 and 202, Landranger 148 .
Car Parking: Free car park at Eardisland near the Cross Inn.
Public Transport: Buses from Leominster.
Terrain: Flat walking along a lane and across riverside meadows.
Refreshments: Pubs and café at Eardisland, pubs at Pembridge.

Even by Herefordshire standards, Eardisland is an exceptionally pretty village, with a large number of timber-framed buildings. Some of these are further enhanced by their attractive setting close to the River Arrow. By the start is the eighteenth century dovecote, now a heritage centre with various exhibitions on local history. Nearby is the medieval church. The Norman nave was built in the twelfth century and the chancel added in the fourteenth century. The original fifteenth century tower collapsed in 1728 and was replaced by the present one shortly afterwards.

Turn right out of the car park ❶ along the road towards the bridge over the River Arrow and take the first lane on the left just before reaching the bridge. Follow it around a left bend and keep along this quiet, winding lane for the next 1¾ miles (2.8km), enjoying the open and extensive views on both sides.

At the gate to a house called Twyford where the lane bends right, ❷ keep ahead along a tarmac drive and at a public footpath sign just before the drive curves left, go through a gate on the right and walk diagonally across a field to a stile on the far side. Climb it, keep in the same direction across the next field

The picturesque village of Eardisland

and cross a footbridge in the far left corner. Continue across the next field and climb a stile onto a road.

Turn left and cross the bridge over the River Arrow. (3) At this point the route continues to the left along a track by the river but it is worthwhile to keep ahead to the crossroads in the centre of Pembridge.

In front of you is a fine timber-framed sixteenth century building called Ye Olde Steppes and the steps at the side of it lead up into the churchyard. Pembridge church dates from the fourteenth century but its most unusual feature is the adjoining detached bell tower, probably built in the thirteenth century and structurally related to the stave churches of Norway. Like

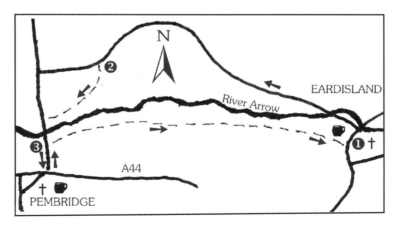

Eardisland, Pembridge has a large number of picturesque black and white buildings, including the Old Market Hall, built around 1520.

Retrace your steps to the bridge over the Arrow ❸ and in front of it turn right along a riverside track, here returning to the main route. After climbing a stile, the way continues in a more or less straight line across the middle of a large expanse of meadowland, making for the hedge in front where you cross a footbridge over a ditch. Walk across the next meadow, climb a stile, keep ahead, climb another stile and continue along a right field edge, veering left to a stile.

After climbing it, head across the next meadow and climb a stile to briefly rejoin the river. Continue across the meadow, making for the far right corner, and just where you enter a belt of woodland, turn right over a double stile. Turn left along the left field edge in the direction of the tower of Eardisland church, climb a stile and bear slightly right across the next field to a plank footbridge.

Cross it, walk across a field, climb a stile, keep ahead and climb one more stile onto a road. Turn left through Eardisland to return to the start.

Pembridge: the medieval church and detatched bell tower

13

A Black and White Village

Around Weobley

The walk starts in one of Herefordshire's well-known black and white villages and explores the pleasant and gently undulating countryside to the south and west of it. There are wide and extensive views all round and for much of the way the tower and spire of Weobley's impressive church is in sight.

Distance: 4½ miles/7.2km.
Approximate Time: 2 hours.
Start: Weobley car park, GR 402517.
Maps: Explorers 201 and 202, Landranger 148 .
Car Parking: Free car park at Weobley near church.
Public Transport: Buses from Hereford.
Terrain: Mainly flat walk along field paths and tracks; some muddy stretches likely after wet weather.
Refreshments: Pubs and cafés at Weobley.

It is no wonder that Weobley is one of the villages on Herefordshire's recommended Black and White Trail as it has a large number of old, picturesque timber-framed buildings. The aptly named Broad Street slopes down from the earthworks of the castle on the south side of the village to the church at the north end. The imposing church, unusually large for a small village, is noted for its tall tower and spire which dominates much of the surrounding

Weobley village

countryside. It dates mainly from the thirteenth and fourteenth centuries and has a Norman south doorway.

Turn left out of the car park ❶ into the village and take the first lane on the left towards Weobley church. Pass to the left of the church and where the lane bends right, turn left through a kissing gate and walk along the left edge of a field. After going through two gates in quick succession, keep along the left edge of the next field, go through a kissing gate and continue along an enclosed path to a road.

Turn left and at a yellow waymark, turn right through a gate and head gently uphill along a hedge-lined track to a stile. Climb it, continue uphill along a right field edge, do not go through the gate in the corner but turn left to keep along the top right edge of the field. Turn right over the next stile and continue along the right field edge over the brow of a hill to a stile. Climb it, descend steps and keep ahead across the next field – later by a hedge on the left – to a stile.

After climbing it, walk along a left field edge, climb two stiles in quick succession, keep along the right edge of the next field and go through a gate onto a tarmac track in front of a large timber-framed farmhouse. Walk along the track, go through a gate, cross a track, go through another gate and keep ahead along an enclosed track. Continue along the left edge of a field, climb a

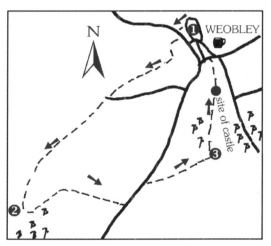

stile in the corner, cross a plank footbridge and head across the next field, veering right to the corner of a hedge. Keep by the hedge on the left, go through a gap between two trees and walk along the left edge of the next field to a footpath post on the edge of woodland. ❷

Turn left along a track and at a yellow waymark, the track bears left away from the edge of the wood to continue along a left field edge to a T-junction. Turn right along an enclosed track to a road, turn left and after about a quarter of a mile (0.4km), turn right along a track, at a public footpath sign. Continue along the right edge of a field and at a crossways – where you see a waymarked kissing gate on the right – turn left ❸ and follow a track straight across the field towards the spire of Weobley church. Go through a kissing gate and bear slightly right across the next field, making for another kissing gate on the far side. After going through that one,

All that remains of Weobley Castle

the route continues through the earthworks of the now vanished Weobley Castle and by a line of old trees on the right to a gate.

Only earthworks remain of the motte and bailey castle built by the De Lacy family, probably around the end of the eleventh century. Originally built of wood, it seems to have been rebuilt in stone in the early thirteenth century but the castle soon fell into ruin and all the later stonework has disappeared. It was one of many castles built by the Norman lords in this turbulent Welsh Border area.

Approaching Weobley

Go through, keep ahead into Weobley and walk down the wide village street. Follow the road to the left in front of the Red Lion to return to the car park.

14

The Town of Books

Hay-on-Wye

A short walk southwards along Offa's Dyke Path leads up the slopes of a hill to a fine viewpoint over the town, Wye valley and surrounding Border country. This is followed by a descent first along a lane and later through a narrow, enclosed, tree-lined valley. The final stretch is a pleasant stroll by the banks of the River Wye.

Distance: 3½ miles/5.6km
Approximate Time: 1½ hours
Start: Hay-on-Wye car park, GR 228423
Maps: Explorers 201 or OL13, Landranger 161
Car Parking: Large pay car park at Hay-on-Wye
Public Transport: Buses from Hereford and Brecon
Terrain: Fairly easy ascent and descent on field paths and a lane, with a final stretch beside the river
Refreshments: Pubs and cafés at Hay-on-Wye

Almost everywhere that you look in Hay-on-Wye there are books. It is impossible to escape them: second hand bookshops are every few yards and bookshelves line the narrow streets and occupy the castle grounds. There are also a fair number of pubs and cafes in the town to serve the large number of visitors who come to this Mecca for booklovers. All this began in 1961 when Richard Booth, later the self-styled 'King of Hay', bought the ruined castle and opened his first second hand bookshop. Since then the enterprise has considerably expanded and turned Hay into one of the foremost second hand and antiquarian book selling centres in the world.

Away from the books, the castle is a reminder that Hay is a Border town and although situated on the east bank of the River Wye, it lies just in Wales. Given its vulnerable location right on the border, it is not surprising that Hay Castle suffered frequent attacks from both English and Welsh during the many wars and skirmishes and was destroyed on a number of occasions. Most of what survives today belongs to an early seventeenth century Jacobean mansion constructed within the walls but this also fell into ruin.

Turn right out of the car park **❶** along the road and at an Offa's Dyke Path sign, turn right down a walled track. Go through a kissing gate, walk along the left edge of a field, and after going through another kissing gate, the route continues along the right edge of the next field.

Go through a kissing gate in the corner, keep by the left edge of the next two fields and descend to cross a footbridge over a stream. Head uphill through trees, go through a gate and continue over the brow of the hill to a gate, footpath post and junction of paths. Go through the gate, bear right and walk across a field to a waymarked stile on the far side.

Hay on Wye: ruined castle and second-hand books

Climb it and turn right down a lane, **❷** curving first left and then right, and continuing more steeply down to a public footpath sign to The Werns, where another lane joins from the left. Turn left along a tarmac track and where the track curves left, keep ahead through a gate and continue up over the brow of a hill. After going through a kissing gate, head across a field, veering right to a waymarked gate in the right hand corner. Go through, walk across the next field, go through a kissing gate in the far right corner and turn sharp right along a track to a gate.

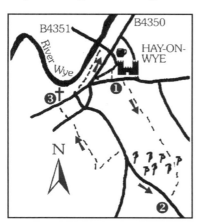

Go through, cross a footbridge over Login Brook and continue downhill along the sunken track through the narrow wooded valley, recrossing the brook several times. Eventually the track becomes a tarmac one and continues down to a road. Turn left and by a sign for Oakland Villas, turn right along a straight, enclosed tarmac track to another road. **❸** Turn right towards Hay church and just after passing it, turn left along an enclosed path which passes the east end of the church and leads down to the river.

Just before reaching a bridge, bear right to reach the riverside path and turn right to follow the wooded bank of the Wye to Hay Bridge. At a fingerpost in front of the bridge, bear right onto a tarmac track, pass under the bridge and turn right up to a road. Turn left to a T-junction and turn right into Hay town centre. Turn left at the Clock Tower, head up a pedestrianised street towards the castle and turn right along Castle Street. At a footpath sign to Car Park and Tourist Information Centre, turn left along an alley which curves right to emerge onto a road opposite the starting point.

The River Wye near the border town on Hay

15

A Sandstone Fortress

Goodrich Castle and Coppet Hill

From the splendid ruins of Goodrich Castle, a quiet, well-wooded lane descends to the banks of the River Wye at the hamlet of Welsh Bicknor. Then follows a lovely two mile (3.2 km) walk along the riverbank, through woodland and across meadows, before turning away from the river and heading over Coppet Hill. Although a modest height of 617 feet (188 m), the views over the Wye Valley from the top and on the subsequent descent are superb.

Distance: 6½ miles/10.5km.
Approximate Time: 3½ hours.
Start: Goodrich Castle car park, GR SO575196.
Maps: Explorer OL14, Landranger 162.
Car Parking: Pay car park at Goodrich Castle.
Public Transport: Buses from Ross-on-Wye and Monmouth.
Terrain: Lane, riverside and woodland paths, with one fairly steep climb and descent.
Refreshments: Pub at Goodrich, café at Goodrich Castle.

The substantial remains of Goodrich Castle occupy a fine defensive position above the River Wye. Originally founded in the late eleventh century, the castle was rebuilt in stone – the local red sandstone – in the twelfth century. The small Norman keep survives from this castle but is completely overshadowed by the massive curtain walls, three rounded corner towers and a gatehouse built in the thirteenth century by the powerful William Marshall, Earl of Pembroke and his successors. At the same time improved domestic buildings were also added. Despite its proximity to the Welsh border, Goodrich saw little action, apart from a long siege by Parliamentary forces in the Civil War in 1645-46, after which it was slighted i.e. rendered incapable of a future military role. Tel: 01600 890538

Begin by walking back along the castle ❶ drive to the road junction in Goodrich. The Hostelrie Inn is to the right but the route is along the first lane on the left, signposted to Courtfield and Welsh Bicknor. Head uphill and at a fork, take the left hand lane, continuing through woodland which slopes steeply down to the river on the left.

The lane climbs steadily, flattens out and emerges from the trees into a more open landscape. Later it re-enters woodland and starts to descend into the valley. At a fork, take the right hand lower lane which now becomes a track and at a public footpath sign in front of a gate, bear right and head downhill along the left inside edge of woodland to the entrance to the Youth Hostel at Welsh Bicknor. Continue along a narrow path to the right of the track, heading steeply downhill – via steps in places – to a T-junction in Welsh Bicknor. ❷

Turn right and the path continues gently down to the banks of the River Wye. The route follows the riverside path for the next two miles (3.2km), negotiating a series of stiles and gates. Initially the path is tree-lined – in summer parts of it may be overgrown with nettles – but later continues across riverside meadows. In the corner of the last meadow, climb a stile to re-enter woodland and after going through a gate, the way continues across meadows again following the river around a right bend below Coldwell Rocks on the opposite bank.

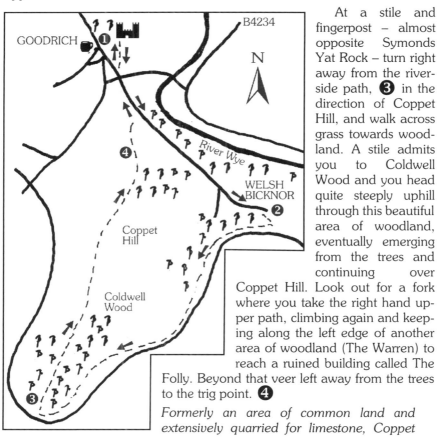

At a stile and fingerpost – almost opposite Symonds Yat Rock – turn right away from the river-side path, ❸ in the direction of Coppet Hill, and walk across grass towards wood-land. A stile admits you to Coldwell Wood and you head quite steeply uphill through this beautiful area of woodland, eventually emerging from the trees and continuing over Coppet Hill. Look out for a fork where you take the right hand up-per path, climbing again and keep-ing along the left edge of another area of woodland (The Warren) to reach a ruined building called The Folly. Beyond that veer left away from the trees to the trig point. ❹

Formerly an area of common land and extensively quarried for limestone, Coppet

Goodrich Castle

Hill was bought by a group of local people in 1985 who set up a trust to manage and conserve it. Previously there were few public rights of way but the trust has opened up some new permissive paths across the hill, including the path used on this walk. It is now a Local Nature Reserve and comprises a mixed terrain of woodland and more open landscapes, the latter mainly covered with trees, bushes and ferns. As the hill is almost enclosed within a horseshoe bend in the Wye, the views on both sides over the valley from the trig point, which stands at a height of 617 feet (188m), are magnificent.

From the trig point bear left and descend quite steeply, plunging into more woodland. Look out for a waymarked post where you turn left down some steps, bear right and continue through the trees, passing several rocky outcrops and zigzagging down to emerge onto a tarmac track. Turn right and after a few yards, turn sharp left onto a lane. Here you rejoin the outward route and retrace your steps to the start.

16

A Classic Viewpoint

Symonds Yat and Mailscot Wood

The walk is easy to follow as most of it is on a well-waymarked Forestry Commission trail. There is little climbing as the route keeps to the high ground above the River Wye and the paths and tracks are gently undulating. Occasional forays into more open country reveal fine views and there are two particularly outstanding views over the Wye Valley: the first near the start and the second at the end, the latter the classic view from the Yat Rock which is generally regarded as one of the finest in the country.

Distance: 4 miles/6.4 km.
Approximate Time: 2 hours.
Start: Symonds Yat Rock, from A40 follow signs to Symonds Yat East, GR SO565159.
Maps: Explorer OL14, Landranger 162.
Car Parking: Forestry Commission pay car park at Symonds Yat Rock.
Public Transport: Occasional buses from Coleford (summer only).
Terrain: Easy route along tracks and paths through woodland.
Refreshments: Café at Symonds Yat Rock

Mailscot Wood, an outlying part of the Royal Forest of Dean, is an attractive mixture of conifer and broadleaved trees and from several points there are grand views over the Wye. In the Middle Ages, Dean was one of a large number of royal hunting grounds that were spread throughout England and occupied the triangle of land roughly between the present Gloucester to Ross-on-Wye road and the Severn and Wye estuaries. Although covering a smaller area nowadays, it is still one of the best-preserved and most extensive forests in England with substantial stretches of thick oak and beech woodland surviving amongst newer conifer plantations. It also has a long industrial history as a quarrying, iron producing and coal mining area but the quarries, iron sites and mines have now almost entirely disappeared and many of the former railway lines built to serve them in the nineteenth century

The classic view over the Wye Valley from Symonds Yat Rock

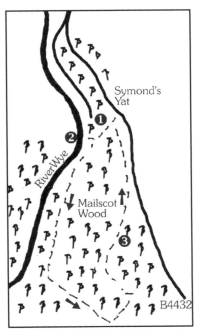

have been converted into footpaths and cycle tracks. Today it is a Forest Park used mainly for leisure and recreational pursuits.

The walk starts in the main car park ❶ at a fingerpost and information boards in front of the toilet block. Facing the block, turn left, in the Mailscot Trail direction, following the regular red-topped posts. Initially you head gently downhill and where a post directs you to turn left, keep ahead, in the direction of a Viewpoint signpost, for a brief detour to a superb viewpoint over the River Wye. ❷

Return to the viewpoint sign and turn right to continue downhill on the winding, red-waymarked circuit, looking out for the frequent marker posts. After curving left, you head uphill along a rocky path and pass through a fence gap to a T-junction.

Looking down on the River Wye from Mailscot Wood

Turn right along a track and at the next T-junction, turn left and continue uphill again. Look out for where a red-topped post directs you to turn left onto a narrow path which winds through the trees to a T-junction. Turn sharp right along a track, at the next marker post turn sharp left onto a path and keep an eye out for where a red-topped post indicates a right turn. Follow another winding path to a T-junction and turn right along a track.

Bear left on meeting another track, ❸ now joining a public right of way, and follow yellow arrows for the remainder of the walk. Cross a tarmac drive, keep ahead, cross another drive and continue along a path which curves left and runs parallel to a road on the right. Walk through a parking area to a fingerpost at a T-junction, turn right, passing the café, and follow signs to the famous viewpoint.

Symonds Yat Rock is a well-known and much photographed viewpoint on the limestone cliffs that rise 394 feet (120m) above a gorge of the River Wye. It is easy to see why the scene from here over the Wye Valley, looking across the Herefordshire lowlands towards the hills of Wales, has delighted generations of visitors. The first people who popularised it were wealthy aristocrats and the Romantic intellectuals of the early nineteenth century who were attracted to this area by the dramatic scenery and picturesque ruins, such as Goodrich Castle and

Tintern Abbey, in the locality. Later the Wye Valley Railway and main roads brought more middle and working class visitors and nowadays the M5 and M50 motorways make the area even more accessible.

On the short walk back to the start from here you pass through the earthworks of a prehistoric fort. This was built in the Iron Age, around 2,500 years ago, and was one of many built on prominent hill tops throughout the country. Now it is surrounded by trees but at the time it was built, it would have commanded extensive views into Wales.

Retrace your steps to the fingerpost and continue past it to return to the start, looking out for the earthworks of the Iron Age fort.

In Mailscot Wood

17

Grand Views from a Broad Ridge

Ewyas Harold Common and Abbey Dore

A short, sharp climb out of the village brings you onto the broad, open and breezy ridge of Ewyas Harold Common. From here the all-round views are both superb and extensive. An invigorating walk along the ridge is followed by a gentle descent into Abbey Dore in the Golden Valley and a pleasant stroll by the river brings you to Dore Abbey. From here you climb back up on to the common and retrace your steps to Ewyas Harold.

Distance: 4 miles/6.4km
Approximate Time: 2 hours
Start: Ewyas Harold, bridge over Dulas Brook, GR SO387286
Maps: Explorer OL13, Landranger 161
Car Parking: Roadside parking in Ewyas Harold near the bridge and the two pubs
Public Transport: Infrequent buses from Hereford
Terrain: Two moderate climbs onto a ridge, paths and tracks over open hilltop, across fields and by a river
Refreshments: Pubs at Ewyas Harold, pub about a 300 yard (274m) detour southwards along the road from Dore Abbey, tea room at Abbey Dore Court Garden (when open)

Looking northwards from the bridge you see Ewyas Harold's sturdy-looking thirteenth century church. To the west a little further along the road is the motte of the Norman castle. Although there is little to see, the site of Ewyas Harold Castle is an interesting one as it was one of only four castles in England that predate the Norman Conquest. It was first founded in 1050 by one of Edward the Confessor's Norman favourites but destroyed by Earl Godwin of Wessex two years later. The year after the conquest William Fitz Osbern, Earl of Hereford, refortified it as a motte and bailey castle. It was built of timber and earth and it seems unlikely that it was ever later rebuilt in stone as most castles were. By the fifteenth century it was largely redundant and fell into disuse and ruin.

Facing the church from the bridge ❶ over Dulas Brook, turn right and take the road on the left (School Road) that bisects the two village pubs. At a T-junction, go up the steps in front, climb a stile and head quite steeply uphill to another stile in the left hand corner of the field. Climb it, continue uphill along the left edge of the next field and turn left over a stile near the top corner.

Walk along a path which curves first right and then left and continues high above the Dulas valley to emerge onto a track. At a junction of tracks a few yards ahead, turn left and at a fork, take the right hand stony track. Where this track bends right, keep ahead along a grassy track across the open expanses of Ewyas Harold Common. The track is not always clear and there are a large number of other paths and tracks on the common which can be confusing but keep in a fairly straight line in a northerly direction, later making for a cottage **❷** – your principal landmark – seen ahead.

Ewyas Harold Common is a broad ridge that mainly comprises open grassland, scrub and gorse. In the past it was quarried and some of the old workings can still be seen. Despite a modest height of 594 feet (181m), the views from the common are magnificent, extending westwards across the Dulas valley to the Black Mountains of south Wales, and looking eastwards over the lush Golden Valley.

The name Golden Valley is believed to be a misnomer. It was called that by the Normans because they thought that the River Dore that flows through the valley was the same as the French d'or (golden). It seems more likely that it was derived from the Welsh word dwr, which means water.

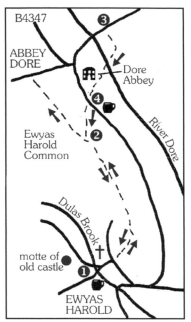

The track curves left in front of the cottage to a junction of tracks. Turn right towards houses and go through a gate to the left of them. As you continue along the top left edge of a sloping field, a lovely view opens up to the right over the Golden Valley, with Dore Abbey seen below.

Climb a ladder stile, continue across a deer enclosure, later by a hedge on the right, then head down and climb another ladder stile to exit the enclosure. Keep ahead along a track and where it curves right, go through a gate, walk across a field and go through another gate onto a lane. Turn right downhill into the hamlet of Abbey Dore. Turn left at a T-junction and the lane curves right. Cross a bridge over the River Dore and just after passing Abbey Dore Court Garden (open from April to

Dore Abbey

September, Tel: 01981 240419), turn right, at a public footpath sign, along an enclosed track. ❸

Where the track veers left to a high gate, keep ahead through a kissing gate and walk along an enclosed path. The path bends right by a high wire fence on the left, then bends left beside the Dore and bends right again to cross a footbridge over the river. Bear slightly left across a field towards the abbey, go through a kissing gate and keep ahead, passing through two more kissing gates in quick succession to enter the abbey churchyard.

Today Dore Abbey is but a fragment of the great medieval monastery that stood on this site. All that is left is the east end and transepts of the abbey church. It was founded as a Cistercian abbey in 1147 and dissolved on the orders of Henry VIII and Thomas Cromwell in 1536. The long nave, 250 feet (76m) in length, was demolished but after a century of neglect, the surviving remains were restored by the local Scudamore family in the 1630s. This is when the present tower was built. Although a fragment, the abbey is one of those strangely atmospheric buildings and the chancel is a particularly beautiful example of thirteenth century architecture.

Pass to the left of the church, walk along a path and go through the lych gate onto the road. ❹ There is a pub – the Neville Arms – about 300 yards

(274m) to the left. The route continues up the steps and over the stile opposite. Bear left and head steeply uphill across a field to a stile in the top left corner. Climb it and continue uphill in the same direction across the next field to another stile. Do not climb that one but turn right along the left field edge, go through a hedge gap and continue uphill by the left edge of the next field, curving left to climb a stile.

Walk along an enclosed path which bends right and after climbing a stile, you emerge onto Ewyas Harold Common again. Bear left along a grassy track – here rejoining the outward route – and at a junction of tracks turn left. In front of the cottage ❷ follow the grassy track to the right and retrace your steps to the start.

The ruins of Tintern Abbey
Walk 18

18

Views That Inspired a Poet and Painter

Tintern Abbey, River Wye and the Devil's Pulpit

If you can only manage to do one walk from this book, try to make it this one as it has both outstanding historic appeal and scenic quality. J.M.W.Turner painted one of his greatest landscapes here in 1795 and William Wordsworth wrote one of his finest poems, Lines Composed a Few Miles above Tintern Abbey, a few years later. This walk will reveal why both men – and many others – were so inspired. The setting of the abbey on the west bank of the Wye is superb and the walk through the valley by the river reveals a series of highly attractive views, which become more spectacular after you climb onto the eastern ridge and continue along a particularly outstanding stretch of Offa's Dyke Path to Brockweir Bridge. Take your time and pick a fine day in order to enjoy this walk to the full.

Distance: 7 miles/11.3km.
Approximate Time: 3½ hours.
Start: Old Station Tintern, off A466 about a quarter of a mile (400m) south of Brockweir Bridge, GR SO537007.
Maps: Explorer OL14, Landranger 162 .
Car Parking: Pay car park at the Old Station Tintern.
Public Transport: Buses from Chepstow and Monmouth.
Terrain: Riverside paths, steep climb through woodland, rocky ridge path.
Refreshments: Pubs and cafés at Tintern, pub at Brockweir, café at Tintern Old Station.

The Old Station at Tintern has been retained as an attractive and interesting visitor centre with a café in the former station building, picnic area, signal box and some old railway carriages that house an information centre, shop and exhibition about the Wye Valley Railway. The line, which opened in 1876, ran along the side of the valley from Monmouth to Chepstow and proved to be extremely popular because of the dramatic scenery along the route. The inevitable decline in passenger traffic after World War II led to its closure in 1964 but parts of the former track have been converted into a footpath, stretches of which are used on this walk. Tel: 01291 689566

Start on the former platform facing the signal box ❶, turn right, walk across a picnic area and continue along a tree-lined track. At a Wye Valley Walk sign, bear right down steps, turn left at the bottom, go through a gate, turn right through another gate and walk along a riverside path.

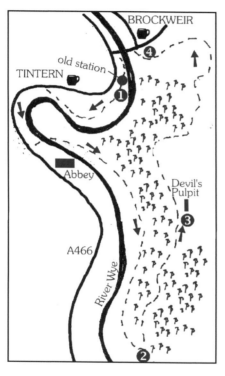

After going through a gate, the path passes through Tintern church-yard and continues up to a road. Turn left through Tintern and follow the river around a left bend, crossing and recrossing the road to make use of the pavements. Keep ahead if visiting Tintern Abbey but the route takes the first turning on the left, signposted to Caswell Wood and Brockweir, and crosses a footbridge over the River Wye, here entering England. Walk along a tree-lined track – part of the former Wye Valley Railway – which curves right and keeps parallel to the river, giving occasional glimpses of the abbey ruins through gaps in the trees on the right.

The two outstanding features of Tintern Abbey are the quality and completeness of the ruins themselves and its magnificent setting on the west (Welsh) bank of the River Wye, almost enclosed by the steep wooded hillsides that rise on both sides. The abbey was founded in 1131 by Walter de Clare, Lord of Chepstow and the remote and secluded location was ideal for the Cistercian monks. Unusually the cloister and domestic buildings are on the north side of the church rather than the sunnier and more sheltered south side, probably because of the nature of the site. The abbey church is the chief glory of Tintern, standing to it full height and almost complete apart from roofs and windows. It dates from a comprehensive rebuilding in the thirteenth century and is an outstanding example of Gothic architecture, particularly noted for the delicate window tracery on the ornate west front. Despite its location

The starting point of the walk

right on the English-Welsh border, the abbey seems to have had a largely uneventful history until its dissolution by Henry VIII and Thomas Cromwell in the 1530s. Tel: 01291 689251

Continue along the track and after nearly two miles (3.2km) you reach a fork. ❷ Take the left hand upper track which climbs steadily and curves left to a T-junction. Turn left along a track which continues uphill to another T-junction and continue along the narrow path opposite – there is a half-hidden yellow-waymarked post – which climbs steeply through dense woodland to a T-junction. Turn left and at a waymarked post, turn right up steps and follow a winding, rocky path steeply uphill, joining Offa's Dyke Path. At the top continue along a twisting and undulating path which keeps along the top of the wooded ridge to the superb viewpoint called the Devil's Pulpit. ❸

From this gap in the trees, the view over the Wye Valley, looking across to the thickly wooded slopes on the Welsh side of the river and with the abbey ruins below, is magnificent. This spot is called the Devil's Pulpit because, according to legend, the devil used to stand here and try to tempt the monks of Tintern away from their duties and monastic vows.

Continue past the viewpoint and look out for where an Offa's Dyke Path post directs you to turn sharp left, just before reaching a kissing gate. Go down some steps and continue through the trees, soon heading steadily downhill to a crossways and fingerpost. Keep ahead, in the Brockweir and St Briavels direction, through the beautiful Caswell Wood, later descending to another crossways by the right edge of the wood. Continue gently downhill along the right inside edge of the trees, climb a stile and keep ahead along the top edge of the woodland until an Offa's Dyke Path post directs you to bear left down a rocky path.

The path soon emerges from the trees and heads diagonally downhill across a field to a stile in the bottom right hand corner. Climb it, descend some steps and continue downhill along a tree-lined path to a fingerpost. Keep ahead, following signs to Brockweir and The Wye, steadily downhill along the left edge of a field to a gate. Go through, continue down a track, going through several gates, to a tarmac drive and turn right to emerge onto a road at Brockweir. ❹

Turn left, cross Brockweir Bridge to re-enter Wales and just before reaching a T-junction, turn left, at a public footpath sign to Tintern, and descend steps. At a fork, keep ahead along a tree-lined track signposted to Old Station Tintern, part of the former railway line, which returns you to the start.

The River Wye near Tintern Abbey

19

Steep Wooded Hillsides
Above the Wye Valley at St Briavels

A quite confusing maze of steep, narrow lanes and footpaths lead from the hilltop village of St Briavels on the edge of the Forest of Dean down to the River Wye, giving outstanding views over the valley. After using some of these to descend to the river near Bigsweir Bridge, a stretch of Offa's Dyke Path takes you steeply up through dense woodland back to the rim of the valley. A final stretch along a quiet lane and through more delightful woodland returns you to the start. This is an energetic walk with steep descents and one steep and lengthy climb. Some of the narrow paths may be overgrown in summer and are likely to be muddy after wet weather.

Distance: 4 miles/6.4km.
Approximate Time: 2½ hours.
Start: St Briavels, by the church and castle gatehouse, GR SO560045.
Maps: Explorer OL14, Landranger 162 .
Car Parking: Roadside parking near church and castle.
Public Transport: Infrequent buses from Monmouth, Chepstow and Coleford.
Terrain: Some steep climbs and descents on narrow lanes and woodland paths.
Refreshments: Pubs at St Briavels.

St Briavels occupies a ridge around 800 feet (244m) high on the fringes of the Forest of Dean overlooking the Wye Valley. Most of its older buildings are grouped in an oval shape around the castle and church. The castle dates from the early thirteenth century when it was used as a hunting lodge by King John. Edward I built the gatehouse in the 1290s as an added defence against possible Welsh raids. Throughout the Middle Ages it was a place of some importance as it served as the administrative and legal centre for the Forest of Dean. It has subsequently been used for a variety of roles, including prison, private residence, school and – currently – a youth hostel. Visitors can enter by the gatehouse and look around the courtyard.

St Briavels church

On the opposite side of the road is the medieval church. It dates from the twelfth century but a new tower was built in 1830 and the building was extensively restored by the Victorians.

Start in front of the castle gatehouse ❶ and facing the church, turn left along the lane. At a fork, take the right hand lower lane, signposted to Lower Meend, and at the next fork, continue downhill along the right hand lane. After a sharp right turn, almost immediately turn sharp left, at a Restricted Byway sign, along a narrow, enclosed path, heading steeply downhill to a track. Bear left, head down a tree-lined path to a narrow lane, turn right and continue steeply downhill.

At a public footpath sign the lane peters out into a track and just before the gates of a sewage works, bear left onto a path through trees to a stile. After climbing it, ford a stream and turn right along the right edge of a field. In the

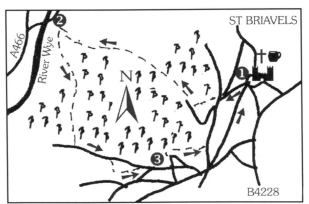

bottom corner, go through a gate and keep ahead along a track which passes to the right of a farm and continues gently downhill. Just before reaching a road near Bigsweir Bridge, turn sharp left onto a track, ❷ here joining the Offa's Dyke Path.

The Gatehouse of St Briavels Castle

Look out for an Offa's Dyke Path sign that directs you to turn left: almost immediately bear right and follow a path diagonally uphill across a field to a gate. Go through, continue in the same direction across the next field and in the top right hand corner, turn right over a stile. Walk across a field towards woodland, go through a gate and continue along a path through the trees. Now comes the most challenging and energetic part of the walk as the path climbs steeply through the dense woodland, twisting and turning – there are occasional waymarks painted on rocks – to the top of the ridge. Just below the top the path bends left and finally climbs steps to a footpath post at a T-junction. Turn right and almost immediately bear left onto a tree-lined, walled path, heading more gently up to emerge onto a lane.

Turn left, passing a large house on the right. After about a quarter of a mile (400m), turn right, at a Restricted Byway sign, along a tree- and hedge-lined path which emerges onto a tarmac track. At another Restricted Byway sign, turn left along an enclosed path to rejoin the lane and turn right. Take the first narrow lane on the left (The Rocks) and at a T-junction, turn left along a track. ❸ Turn right in front of a house, head downhill through the trees, climb a stone stile and descend to a footpath post at a T-junction. Turn right along a most attractive path through steep-sided woodland and eventually you turn left over a footbridge, head up steps to a track and turn left to a lane.

Turn left and after a few yards, turn right up steps, at a public footpath sign, and head steeply uphill through woodland to emerge onto another lane. Turn left and follow it back to St Briavels.

20

A Great Border Stronghold
Chepstow and the Lower Wye Valley

From the castle and walled town of Chepstow, the gateway to Wales, the walk crosses the bridge over the Wye into England and uses short stretches of two long distance paths – the Gloucestershire Way and Offa's Dyke Path – to take you on a pleasant circuit on the eastern side of the Lower Wye Valley. There are views of the Severn estuary and Severn Bridge but the most spectacular view is across a great bend in the Wye at Wintour's Leap.

Distance: 5 miles/8km.
Approximate Time: 2½ hours.
Start: Chepstow, Town Gate at the top of High Street, GR ST532938.
Maps: Explorer OL14, Landranger 162 .
Car Parking: Pay car parks at Chepstow.
Public Transport: Buses from Newport, Monmouth, Gloucester and Lydney; trains from Newport and Gloucester.
Terrain: Undulating route mainly on lanes and field paths.
Refreshments: Pubs ands cafés at Chepstow.

Chepstow is dominated by its superb castle which sprawls over a steep cliff above the Wye. Its strategic location, commanding one of the principal routeways from England into south Wales, was soon realised by the Norman conquerors and less than a year after the Battle of Hastings, William FitzOsbern, Lord of Hereford began its construction. At the time most castles were built of timber and earth and rebuilt in stone later but Chepstow was constructed from stone right from the start making it one of the earliest stone buildings in the country. Although later remodelled, the impressive Norman hall keep, standing at the narrowest point of the castle, survives from the original eleventh century building. In the thirteenth century the castle was considerably enlarged and strengthened by the addition of a gatehouse, strong outer walls and towers. One of the most powerful of these new additions was a tall rounded tower, later named Marten's Tower after Henry Marten, one of the judges who signed Charles I's death warrant. He was imprisoned in it after the accession of Charles II but apparently lived there in some comfort, despite being one of the men directly responsible for the execution of the king's father.

Although one of the largest and most powerful of Border castles, Chepstow saw little action and its only serious military engagement came during the Civil War when it was besieged by Parliamentary forces. Unlike most castles, it was not subsequently dismantled but briefly retained and adapted for artillery warfare. By the end of the seventeenth century it had fallen into ruin but is still more complete than most of Britain's medieval fortresses. Tel: 01291 624065

The town was enclosed on the landward side by walls, substantial stretches of which survive, plus one of the gateways from where the walk starts. The much restored and altered church near the river was originally part of an Augustinian priory also founded by William FitzOsbern in 1071. It was dissolved by Henry VIII in 1536 and suffered much neglect and damage but the nave and a fine Norman west doorway survive from the eleventh century priory.

The Town Gate is the one remaining gateway in Chepstow's Portwall, the medieval wall that was built across the landward side of the town. Start by walking along Welsh Street ❶ and at a footpath sign to Castle and

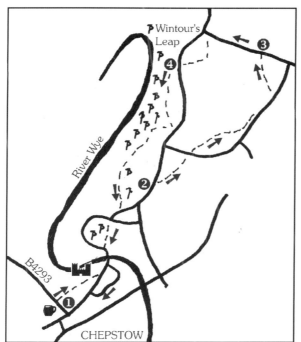

Riverside, turn right through a gate into a recreation area. At a fork, take the left hand lower path which descends below the castle walls and at the bottom, keep ahead through a car park to a road.

Turn left and cross the bridge over the River Wye, here entering England. Where the road bends left, keep ahead, at a Gloucestershire Way sign, along an uphill, tarmac walled path and go up steps onto the road again. Cross over, walk along a short stretch of tarmac path and continue along a lane to a road. Keep ahead, take the first road on the right (Elm Road) and where it bears right, turn left, ❷ at a public footpath sign, along a narrow enclosed path. From here there are fine views over the Severn estuary.

The Town Gate of Chepstow
The main gateway in the town's medieval walls

Climb a stone stile, head gently downhill across a field, go through a kissing gate at the bottom and continue uphill across the next field, making for the top right hand corner where you go through a gate onto a lane. Cross over, go through the gate opposite and follow the direction of a public footpath sign diagonally across a field. Go through a hedge gap, maintain the same direction across the next field, passing a redundant stile

Chepstow Castle
Built to guard the English-Welsh border

and continuing on to the corner. Bear right through a gate, walk along a track, go through another gate and turn left uphill along a tree-lined track. After going through two more gates in quick succession, continue along an enclosed track and where it ends, turn right through a gate onto a narrow lane. ❸

The great bend in the River Wye at Wintour's Leap

Turn left and at Gloucestershire Way and public footpath signs, turn left over a stile and bear right across the field corner to a waymarked post. Continue along an uphill path through a small belt of trees and keep by a wire fence on the right to a kissing gate. Go through, keep ahead by a right field edge, go through another kissing gate and continue to a lane. Turn left along this pleasant, winding, uphill lane for half a mile (800m) and just before a T-junction, turn sharp left, at an Offa's Dyke Path sign, down a tarmac track.

Where the track ends, keep ahead along a tree-lined path which bears right to enter a field. Turn right along the right field edge which curves left, go through a hedge gap in the corner and turn right along the right edge of the next field. Go through a kissing gate, keep ahead along a narrow enclosed path and go up steps onto a road. Turn right and at an Offa's Dyke Path sign, the route continues to the left ❹ but a brief detour along the road to where it bends right rewards you with the magnificent viewpoint of Wintour's Leap.

This great view over a bend in the River Wye looks across to the steep-sided and thickly-wooded Wynd Cliff. The name comes from Sir John Wintour, a Royalist supporter, who during the Civil War is alleged to have escaped from Parliamentary troops by leaping from this point. Given the height it seems unlikely.

Return to the Offa's Dyke Path sign ❹ and turn right onto a narrow enclosed path from which there is another, rather more precarious view of

Wintour's Leap. Go through a kissing gate, keep head along the path above a deep quarry on the right and bear right to emerge onto a track. Walk along a tree-lined path, go through two kissing gates in quick succession and continue more steeply down another tree-lined path which bends right and emerges onto a road via a gate. Turn right and at an Offa's Dyke Way sign, turn right through a kissing gate and walk along an enclosed path.

Look out for the next sign which directs you to turn left through a kissing gate and walk diagonally across a field to another kissing gate on the far side. Go through, turn right along a track, by a high wall on the left, and just in front of gates, turn left – there is a yellow arrow here – along an enclosed path to a kissing gate. Go through, turn right along a right field edge, go through another kissing gate and turn left through trees.

Continue across the field ahead, passing the remains of a lookout tower, an outlying part of Chepstow's defences, and as you head downhill, there is a grand view over the town. Go through a kissing gate in the bottom left hand corner and turn right along a lane, here rejoining the outward route. Retrace your steps as far as the bridge over the River Wye and after crossing it, keep ahead up Bridge Street into the town centre and continue up to the starting point.

Another view from Wintour's Leap

Index

More walks from the Meridian catalogue

COUNTRY WALKS AROUND THE NATIONAL FOREST by Brian Conduit

The National Forest is an area of 200 square miles covering parts of Leicestershire, Staffordshire and Derbyshire. This collection of twenty walks is not just confined to the boundaries of the National Forest but also includes a number of interesting and attractive areas on its periphery. Among the major attractions are the many woodlands, both new and mature, paths across riverside meadows and along canal towpaths, attractive villages, great parklands, and many sites of historic interest.
£5.95. ISBN 978-1-869922-56-6. 84 pages. 37 illustrations. 20 maps

BEST WALKS IN THE MIDLANDS by Des Wright

This is the fourth collection of walks prepared by Des Wright.The walks are not difficult and are well within the capabilities of the average walker. Some are quite short and so will appeal to those with young families or those who are taking their first steps in exploring the 'great outdoors'. The distances range from 3½ miles to 12 miles. Most can be accessed by public transport and details of suitable services are provided.
£6.95. ISBN-13: 978-1-869922-57-3 120 pages. 38 b/w photos. 20 sketch maps.

RAMBLERS' CHOICE: Some favourite walks in the Midlands. Edited by Peter Groves

In this collection members of the City of Birmingham Group of the Ramblers' Association offer some of their favourite walks in Warwickshire, West Midlands, Worcestershire and Staffordshire. They are not too difficult and many have longer and shorter versions, the longer walks ranging from about 5 miles/8km to 9½ miles/15 km; the shorter walks from about 3 miles/5 km to 7¾ miles/12.5 km.
£5.95. ISBN 978-1-869922-54-2. 96 pages. 31 illustrations. 20 maps

HERITAGE DISCOVERY WALKS IN THE MIDLANDS by Peter Groves

Britain has a rich historical heritage and the twenty-one walks in this book explore some fine Midlands countryside and also present opportunities to visit castles, battlefields, nature reserves, museums, churches and cathedrals, to admire fine architecture and to explore some historic towns.
£6.95. ISBN 1-869922-50-6. 160 pages. 52 illustrations. 20 maps

WALKS AROUND THE MALVERNS by Roy Woodcock

The Malvern Hills and their surroundings provide magnificent opportunities for rambling, and in this book of twenty walks Roy Woodcock explores many of their superb features. The walks cover the entire range of hills and the neighbouring commons, together with some of the delightful countryside nearby. Distances range from two miles to eight miles, plus a leg stretcher of between ten and sixteen miles (depending on the starting point) that takes in the full length of the ridge and ascends all the Malvern peaks.
Second revised edition £6.95. ISBN 1 869922 53 0. 112 pages. 41 illustrations. 20 maps.

A YEAR OF WALKS IN THE THREE CHOIRS COUNTIES by Roy Woodcock

The Three Choirs Counties comprise Herefordshire, Gloucestershire and Worcestershire and this selection of walks takes twelve widely distributed locations, one for each month of the year. Each walk is described for a particular month, but all of them are good for any time of the year.
£7.95. ISBN 1-869922-49-2. 128 pages. 37 illustrations. 20 maps

WALKS IN SEVERN COUNTRY by Roy Woodcock

The River Severn, Britain's longest river, rises in Wales and flows through the beautiful counties of Powys, Shropshire, Worcestershire and Gloucestershire before discharging into the Bristol Channel. In this book the author presents an absorbing account of the geography and history of the river accompanied by twenty walks that explore some of the fine towns

and countryside that the Severn passes through on its 220 mile journey to the sea.
£7.95. ISBN 1-869922-49-2. 128 pages. 37 illustrations. 20 maps

WALKING WITH THE FAMOUS … AND THE INFAMOUS by Roger Seedhouse

A unique book of fifteen walks in Shropshire through areas associated with some of the county's most colourful historical characters. In an original and distinctive style the walks also relate the principal events of the character's lives and are written as if through their own eyes.
£7.95. ISBN 1-869922-46-8. 128 pages. 15 maps. Illustrated with photos and drawings.

WARWICKSHIRE WALKS TO WET YOUR WHISTLE by Roger Seedhouse

Following his two highly successful books, Walks to Wet your Whistle and More Walks to Wet your Whistle, Roger Seedhouse now presents a further collection of walks, all with good pubs, in Warwickshire – a land of lakes and country parks which are a delight to behold, merging into the Northern Cotswolds with its buildings of honey-hued stone.
£8.95. ISBN 1-869922-48-4 120 pages 21 photos 20 maps

WALKS IN WARWICKSHIRE AND WORCESTERSHIRE by Des Wright

This third collection of walks by a popular author explores further some of the attractive countryside in two West Midlands counties. The walking is not difficult, mostly on the flat and with no strenuous climbs. The walks are all circular and can be reached easily by car and, with one exception, by public transport. Distances range between 2 and 9.5 miles, with one rather more strenuous walk of l4 miles.
£6.95. ISBN 1-869922-44-1. 112 pages. 24 illustrations. 22 maps.

THE ELAN VALLEY WAY by David Milton

The Elan Valley Way runs from Frankley, on the western fringe of Birmingham, to the Elan Valley in mid-Wales. It is loosely based around the course followed by the Elan Valley aqueduct along which Birmingham's water supply has passed since 1904. Largely following footpaths and bridleways, and with many superb views, the 128½ mile route passes through some delightful walking areas in the counties of Worcestershire, Shropshire, Herefordshire and Powys.
£7.95. ISBN 1 869922 39 5. 160 pages. 21 photographs. 21 maps.

A TEME VALLEY WALK by David Milton

The Teme is one of the most beautiful and fast-flowing rivers in the country but remains quite secretive for much of its length. This long distance walk remains as dose as possible to the river but takes to the hills where footpaths, public transport or accommodation needs dictate. It starts in Worcester and ends, after visiting the source of the river, in Newtown, a total distance of 93 miles.
£8.95. ISBN 1-869922-45-X. 176 pages. 22 illustrations. 17 maps.

THE RIVERSIDES WAY by David Milton

A 70 mile circular walk in the area of the Welsh Marches immediately to the south and west of Ludlow. Centred on Aymestry it takes in the valleys and surrounding hills of the two rivers that drain the region – the Teme, in the north, and the Lugg, in the south.
£8.95. ISBN 1-869922-43-3. 160 pages. 13 photos. 14 maps.

All Meridian titles are available from booksellers or direct from the publishers.

Please send your remittance, including the following amounts for postage and packing:
Order value up to £10.00 add £1.50;over £10.00 and up to £20.00 add £2.50;
over £20.00 add £3.00.
Meridian Books Sales Office
8 Hartside Close, Lutley, Halesowen, West Midlands B63 1HP Tel: 0121-429 4397
e-mail: meridian.books@tiscali.co.uk
Please send for our complete catalogue of walking guides.